THE SEVERN WAY

THE SEVERN WAY

215 MILES FROM THE RIVER SEVERN'S SOURCE IN POWYS TO SEVERN BEACH NEAR BRISTOL

by Terry Marsh

JUNIPER HOUSE, MURLEY MOSS,
OXENHOLME ROAD, KENDAL, CUMBRIA LA9 7RL
www.cicerone.co.uk

© Terry Marsh 2023
Third Edition 2023
ISBN: 978 1 78631 140 5
Second edition 2019
First edition 2014

Printed in India by Replika Press Pvt Ltd using responsibly sourced paper.
A catalogue record for this book is available from the British Library.
All photographs are by the author unless otherwise stated.

 © Crown copyright 2023. OS PU100012932.

Updates to this Guide

While every effort is made by our authors to ensure the accuracy of guidebooks as they go to print, changes can occur during the lifetime of an edition. Any updates that we know of for this guide will be on the Cicerone website (www.cicerone.co.uk/1140/updates), so please check before planning your trip. We also advise that you check information about such things as transport, accommodation and shops locally. Even rights of way can be altered over time. We are always grateful for information about any discrepancies between a guidebook and the facts on the ground, sent by email to updates@cicerone.co.uk or by post to Cicerone, Juniper House, Murley Moss, Oxenholme Road, Kendal LA9 7RL.

Register your book: To sign up to receive free updates, special offers and GPX files where available, create a Cicerone account and register your purchase via the 'My Account' tab at www.cicerone.co.uk.

Front cover: Poplars and field of gold, Maisemore (Stage 17)

CONTENTS

Map key 6

INTRODUCTION 9
The Severn: Source to sea. 10
About the route 13
Weather and when to go 14
Getting there and transport. 15
Accommodation. 16
Preparation and fitness 17
Equipment 17
Suggested itineraries. 18
Maps and GPS 20
Using this guide 20

POWYS 21
Stage 1   Rhyd-y-benwch to the source 23
Variant start: Eisteddfa Gurig to the source via Plynlimon 27
Stage 2   Source of the Severn to Llanidloes. 29
Stage 3   Llanidloes to Caersws 33
Stage 4   Caersws to Newtown 41
Stage 5   Newtown to Welshpool. 48
Stage 6   Welshpool to Crew Green. 56

SHROPSHIRE. 63
Stage 7   Crew Green to Montford Bridge 65
Stage 8   Montford Bridge to Shrewsbury (English Bridge) 69
Stage 9   Shrewsbury (English Bridge) to Atcham. 75
Stage 10   Atcham to Ironbridge 79
Stage 11   Ironbridge to Bridgnorth 86
Stage 12   Bridgnorth to Upper Arley. 94

WORCESTERSHIRE 102
Stage 13   Upper Arley to Stourport-on-Severn 104
Stage 14   Stourport-on-Severn to Worcester 109
Stage 15   Worcester to Upton-upon-Severn 116
Stage 16   Upton-upon-Severn to Tewkesbury 121

GLOUCESTERSHIRE ... 125

Stage 17	Tewkesbury to Gloucester Docks	127
Stage 18	Gloucester Docks to Upper Framilode	136
Stage 19	Upper Framilode to Frampton-on-Severn	141
Stage 20	Frampton-on-Severn to Sharpness	146
Stage 21	Sharpness to Oldbury-on-Severn	152
Stage 22	Oldbury-on-Severn to Severn Beach	156
Bristol Link:	Severn Beach to Bristol	160

Appendix A Route summary table ... 167
Appendix B Useful contacts ... 169
Appendix C Facilities along the Way ... 171

Route symbols on OS map extracts
(for OS legend see printed OS maps)

- route
- alternative route/detour
- start point
- finish point
- route direction

Features on the overview map

- County/Unitary boundary
- National boundary
- Urban area
- National Park eg **BRECON BEACONS**
- Area of Outstanding Natural Beauty eg *Shropshire Hills*
- 800m / 600m / 400m
- 200m / 75m / 0m

Acknowledgements

It is perfectly feasible to compile a guidebook such as this by simply starting at the beginning and continuing to the end, writing as you go. Logical as that might seem, logistically, such an approach can be a recipe for disaster; it's okay on middle-distance trails, but on anything longer you need teamwork and/or extensive planning; just as you would on doing the walk itself.

On the local authority side, I had the assistance of a team of officers working for the individual county councils along the route, and they offered helpful advice and kindly read the finished manuscript for their respective sections. Any errors that remain, however, are my responsibility.

From a practical point of view, writing such a guide as this is made so much easier by using a two-car approach, shuttling backwards and forward from start to day's end, but always making forward progress. It works when doing the walk, too.

My brother-in-law Jon accompanied me throughout the entire journey, while my son's car came into play once Bridgnorth was reached. To both I am grateful for the endless running about they did, even giving the appearance of enjoying it; they certainly put the real ales en route through their paces.

My wife, Vivienne, also joined us for stretches, but we both missed our faithful companion, Teal, who sadly died during the compilation of the book; she would have loved the walk, just as any dog would. So, I dedicate this book to the memory of Teal; she'll always be with us.

The Severn from the Miners' Bridge, Highley, Shropshire

INTRODUCTION

The Severn at Buildwas, Shropshire

Flowing through superb landscapes and passing appealing towns and villages, the River Severn pulls together threads of history, trade, commerce, civil war and the lives of ordinary folk to produce a tapestry that is finely woven and rich in colour. That walkers should want to trace its course, its many twists and turns, is hardly surprising, not least because of its capacity to offer countless challenges and plentiful delights.

As our pace of life has become increasingly frenetic, walking the Severn Way is a chance to get away from it all and relax without having to resort to distant mountain regions. The Way offers a unique experience combining the simple joy of being out in the country air to the sense of well-being that comes from exploring the history and heritage of a remarkable group of counties, towns and villages.

For most of its route in close company with the river, this route is a lesson in historical geography brought vividly to life, one that builds on the concepts learned at school about a river's journey from source to sea with a demonstration of mankind's impact on the landscapes through which the river flows.

THE SEVERN WAY

THE SEVERN: SOURCE TO SEA

The river (in Welsh: Afon Hafren, although its Latin name, Sabrina, crops up from time to time) is the longest river in the UK, at about 354km (220 miles), and the second longest in the British Isles, after Ireland's River Shannon. It rises at an altitude of 610m (2001 feet) on Plynlimon (Ceredigion), near Llanidloes (Powys), in the Cambrian Mountains of mid-Wales. It then flows through Shropshire, Worcestershire, Gloucestershire and South Gloucestershire, with the county towns of Shrewsbury, Worcester and Gloucester on its banks. The Severn is the greatest river in terms of water flow in England and Wales.

The birthplace of a river is an imprecise location; in the case of the Severn it is 'officially' marked by a large pole standing forlorn and often mist-shrouded amid acres of sphagnum bog. Yet it is evident that water is draining into this infant river from higher on Plynlimon's slopes. It is an eerie and lonely place, a far cry from the urban and rural pastures to come. Here, the tang of wild places and the call of upland birds sharpen the appetite for the journey.

Only a short way from its sluggish start, the Severn has gathered force and bustles through the greenness of the Hafren Forest and the confining valleys below before spreading out and slowing its pace as it passes through the agricultural pasturelands of mid-Wales. In the Powys stages of the Way, especially after Llanidloes, the river is frequently viewed at a

The boggy landscape near the source of the Severn, Powys

THE SEVERN: SOURCE TO SEA

distance rather than close up, as will be the case later on. For the walker, this is the most demanding part of the route and the most varied, with many trying ups and downs.

By the time the route enters Shropshire (and England) at Crew Green, the river has grown into a meandering watercourse that cuts through the county's floodplains, chiselling steep banks lined with alder and willow. On the approach to Ironbridge, the character change is quite noticeable as the river bullies its way through the gorge before easing southwards through well-wooded landscapes that lead on to Bewdley, Stourport and Worcester.

Now the river takes on another character, busy with boats and anglers, as it presses southwards to Tewkesbury and Gloucester. But it has not altogether lost its force, as the distinctive cliffs at Wainlode demonstrate. Once beyond Gloucester, the river becomes tidal, and has the second highest tidal range in the world. Originally, the Severn was tidal as far as Worcester, and capable of being navigated, with some difficulty, as far as Welshpool.

Around the Arlingham loop it becomes clear that large areas of sand are exposed at low tide, especially west of Frampton-on-Severn, which increasingly are favoured by waders and wildfowl. The grazing meadows near Slimbridge are hugely popular with passage and wintering waders, and the winter grounds for large numbers of white-fronted geese.

Onward now the river is noticeably widening and there is a keen

View across the Severn at Upper Framilode, Gloucestershire

sense that the end of the Way is not far distant, an end that is signalled by two massive bridges that taunt the weary walker. Officially, the Severn Way ends at Severn Beach, a significant moment for those who have come such a long way from the bleak heights of Plynlimon.

THE BRIDGES OF THE SEVERN

The old Atcham Bridge

Throughout its length, the Severn is crossed by numerous bridges, many having replaced ancient ferries. Many of the bridges are notable in their own right, with several designed and built by the engineer Thomas Telford. Among these is the famous Iron Bridge at Ironbridge, the world's first iron arch bridge, while at the far end of the Way stand the two road bridges linking Wales with the southern counties of England: the Severn Bridge, opened in 1966 and carrying what is now the M48, and the Second Severn Crossing, opened in 1996 and carrying the M4 motorway. Before the first bridge in 1966, the channel was crossed by the Aust Ferry.

Other notable bridges include:
- Buttington Bridge, built in 1872
- Montford Bridge, Telford's first ever bridge design, built between 1790 and 1792
- Welsh Bridge in the centre of Shrewsbury, built in 1795
- English Bridge, also in Shrewsbury, designed and completed in 1774 by John Gwynn

ABOUT THE ROUTE

- Atcham Bridges, the old one built in 1774, the newer, carrying the B4380, in 1929
- Albert Edward Bridge in Coalbrookdale, a rail bridge opened in 1864
- Coalport Bridge, like that in Ironbridge, made of cast iron, and built in 1818
- Bewdley Bridge, another designed by Telford, completed in 1798
- Holt Fleet Bridge in Worcestershire, also from the engineering genius of Thomas Telford, opened in 1828
- Upton town bridge, built as recently as 1940, and the only bridge to cross between Worcester and Tewkesbury
- Queenshill Viaduct, which carries the M50 between Junctions 1 and 2
- Mythe Bridge, north of Tewkesbury, another Telford bridge, opened in April 1826
- Haw Bridge, a steel beam bridge, south of Tewkesbury
- Maisemore Bridge north of Gloucester, which carries the A417 and is a single masonry arch, dating to 1230
- Over Bridge, a single masonry arch built by Telford
- Over Rail Bridge, the last bridge before the Old Severn Crossing, 30 miles downstream

ABOUT THE ROUTE

Over the years there have been a number of small changes to the route of the Way that affect the overall distance. Recently, the latest mapping technology has been used to measure distances and height changes far more accurately.

From the source to Severn Beach, the distance is 344km (215 miles), and, perhaps surprisingly for a route that follows a river downwards, involves 2740m (8985ft) of ascent (much of it in small undulations), as well as the expected quantity of descent (3340m/11,000ft). In addition, there is the walk up to the source, which involves a further 5.5km (3½ miles) along with 340m (1120ft) of ascent, and 65m (210ft) of descent.

An alternative start has been introduced from Eisteddfa Gurig,

Severn Way waymark

The 'new' line of the Way, near Clifton, Gloucestershire

which may be of interest to strong walkers. This is not part of the Severn Way, and is not waymarked, but its purpose is twofold: to avoid repeating the route between Rhyd-y-benwch and the source; and to acknowledge Plynlimon Fawr and its massif not only as the source of the river about to be followed, but as the source of a number of other rivers of regional and national importance. This addition measures 8.9km (5½ miles), with ascent of 420m (1380ft) and descent of 250m (815ft). That takes the route only as far as the source, with a good measure of walking still remaining to get down to Llanidloes.

This information has been arrived at by a combination of methods which means that, although the distances cited are accurate, the figures for ascent and descent are not as precise. In fact, although there are a number of places where uphill work is necessary, in the main, once the first three days are completed, then the general characteristic is of level walking.

WEATHER AND WHEN TO GO

Choosing the best time to tackle the Severn Way is never going to be easy, for reasons that affect few other long-distance routes. Notably, the river has a propensity to flood, something that causes significant damage to adjoining properties – the sight of large caravans on stilts is a regular if slightly bizarre feature along the route. In 1947, the Severn reached its highest recorded levels, and flooding cost the towns along the river over £12 million. Shrewsbury was completely cut off from the rest of the world, truly 'islanded in Severn stream', as the poet AE Housman put it. Shops and businesses were affected and people had to walk over wooden boards to cross the flooded area. At a number of places along the Way there are signs indicating the flood levels in certain years; it's a sobering thought to realise that the river level at times can be three feet over your head.

For the walker, once the floods have subsided and for some time afterwards, there can be a residue of slippery, glutinous mud studded with tree branches and river debris, which makes some stretches very tiring, especially north and south of Worcester.

Overall, the best months are those between May and September, but an intensely cold snap at any time of year, one that freezes the ground, may warrant a few days' skirmish with the route, if not with the entire walk.

The early stages of the walk experience mountain weather, which steadily eases as the river is followed southwards. But what is not instantly obvious is that the general trend of the route is directly into the prevailing winds and this, too, can be another tiring factor. In hot conditions, there are many days when there is very little shelter from the sun.

You can get some indication of conditions by checking the weather forecast both the day before you go and again on the morning you intend to walk. There are reliable sources of weather information on the internet, notably:

- www.bbc.co.uk/weather: this site allows you to set your favourite locations, in order to obtain a more specific forecast
- www.metoffice.gov.uk (the Met Office's own website)

These sites are also available as a free apps for use on iPhones, iPads and other smartphones.

GETTING THERE AND TRANSPORT

To access the beginning of the Severn Way, Rhyd-y-benwch car park and picnic site is 9.7km (6 miles) west of Llanidloes. It can also be reached from the northern end of Llyn Clywedog on minor roads. The nearest railway station is at Caersws, from where it is about a 20-minute bus ride to Llanidloes.

On reaching the end of the Way at Severn Beach, the quickest way to Bristol is by train. If you have more time on your hands, the Severn Way Bristol Link takes you there on foot, switching the Severn for the Avon (see Bristol Link: Severn Beach to Bristol at the end of the main route description). From the main railway station at Bristol Temple Meads there are direct services available to London, Scotland, Wales, Manchester and Birmingham. National Express coach services (www.nationalexpress.com) operate from the Bristol bus station to cities across the UK. Megabus (www.uk.megabus.com) operates coaches from Bristol to London and Cwmbran, and Greyhound

The Severn Way

One way to travel: In 2012, Southern Railway 'Battle of Britain' class No 34053 'Sir Keith Park' returned to service on the Severn Valley Railway, after a 47-year layoff

(www.greyhounduk.com) operates from Bristol Airport to Swansea.

There is little difficulty getting to any of the start and finish points of walking days, and all the main towns and many of the villages are well served by public transport. Whether you can time your arrival to coincide with public transport is, however, another matter, and largely depends on the logistics of your walking plan.

Information about public transport in each of the counties is available from their respective websites (see Appendix B) and from Traveline (0871 200 2233 www.traveline.info).

ACCOMMODATION

All the towns and villages that feature as start or end points of walk sections have some form of accommodation, from inns and hotels to B&Bs and campsites. But there is no one source of information about accommodation along the route, which means that careful planning is necessary.

Information about accommodation (but not specifically for the Severn Way) is available as follows:
- Powys: www.midwalesmyway.com
- Shropshire: www.shropshiretourism.co.uk/where-to-stay.html
- Worcestershire: www.visitworcestershire.org/stay
- Gloucestershire: www.thecityofgloucester.co.uk/accommodation
- South Gloucestershire: www.southglos.gov.uk
- Bristol: www.visitbristol.co.uk

You may have more success searching specifically for a town or village, for example typing in 'Llanidloes' to find www.llanidloes.com, which provides a list of hotels, inns, B&Bs and so on. The tourist information offices listed in Appendix B will also provide local information.

PREPARATION AND FITNESS

Fit, healthy and experienced walkers accustomed to long days on the hills will encounter no difficulty in tackling the Severn Way, but it would be foolish even to think about setting off if you have not previously done any rough walking or carried a heavy pack. Getting yourself into condition is neither an arduous nor an unpleasant process, and every walk you do in preparation will make your experience and enjoyment of the Way all the better.

Nor does conditioning extend only to you. It is vitally important, for example, that you avoid wearing new boots that are not broken in or clothing that has not had the chance to lose its newness. Comfort on a long walk can be critically important; discomfort can be painful if allowed to go on too long. If you feel blisters coming on, or your boots start rubbing around the ankles, do attend to the problem sooner rather than later.

EQUIPMENT

All walkers have their own preferences in the matter of equipment and clothing. When extending day walking into multiple day walking much the same general items are needed, with the emphasis on being able to stay warm and dry (as much as possible), and comfortable in all weather conditions.

The following list may be found a useful reminder:
- rucksack (comfortable, well padded, appropriate to backpacking rather than day walking, and preferably already used by you, if only on trial walks)
- boots
- socks (and spare socks)
- trousers (or shorts, but not shorts alone)
- underclothes
- shirt
- mid-layer (for example, pullover) and spare, wind- and waterproof jacket and overtrousers
- hat
- gloves
- maps
- compass
- torch (with spare battery and bulbs)
- whistle
- first aid kit
- survival bag or space blanket
- food and drink
- insect repellent
- wash kit, including half a roll of toilet tissue (for emergencies)
- small hand towel

Pedal bin liners have a number of useful purposes: keeping wet clothes separate from dry in the sack, containing burst packets of food, cereal and so on and rubbish, until a suitable

THE SEVERN WAY

Some characters met along the Way

disposal point can be reached, and for insulating dry socks from wet boots when walking.

Take a notebook and keep a personal record of your experiences, or a book to read.

Given the proximity of towns and large villages, there is ample opportunity to get hold of cash and to replenish supplies. Appendix C gives a list of facilities along the way, but do not rely on maps as an indicator of the location of pubs, for example, as many have closed down in recent years. Where pubs exist at the moment they are mentioned in the route description.

SUGGESTED ITINERARIES

For a walk that can take more than three weeks, it is impossible to give meaningful itineraries; much will depend on the individual's ability

Suggested Itineraries

and the amount of walking they are comfortable with in a day. There is, however, much to be said for tackling the Way over a number of visits, not trying to do the entire thing in one go.

For example, for logistical reasons, during the preparation of this book, four visits were made; two in September and two in April. They ran from Source to Shrewsbury; Shrewsbury to Bridgnorth; Bridgnorth to Tewkesbury; Tewkesbury to Severn Beach (plus the Bristol link).

Appendix A provides a route summary table, to enable the reader to fashion their own itinerary more easily. The breakdown it shows produces an average daily walk of just over 16km (10 miles), which, at a leisurely pace, is perfectly adequate and allows for exploration.

Clockwise from top left: lady's smock; cowslips; sloes on blackthorn; bullrush

MAPS AND GPS

To cover the entire walk, the following maps are required:
- OS Landranger: 126, 127, 135, 136, 138, 150, 162, 172
- OS Explorer: 14, 154, 155, 167, 179, 190, 204, 214, 215, 216, 218, 219, 240, 241, 242

There is an increasing number of satellite-linked GPS systems on the market these days, some of which contain the mapping you need for given counties or long-distance trails. The precision of these significantly reduces the risk of error, and they are very reliable guides in poor visibility.

They are, however, no substitute for the ability to read conventional mapping or for possessing navigational skills, but for some years the author has been confidently using a Satmap Active 10, with appropriate 1:25,000 mapping on SD cards. SD mapping for the counties of Powys, Shropshire, Herefordshire and Worcestershire, Gloucestershire and Avon will be necessary to cover the entire walk.

USING THIS GUIDE

This guide is divided into county-based chapters and each of these counties has its own discernible character in terms of landscape, plants and wildlife. The precise location of the boundary is also noted in the text so that, should have you cause to give feedback to the relevant local authority about the route, you will know which county you are in. This is especially relevant where the section on Gloucestershire embraces both Gloucestershire and South Gloucestershire County Councils.

But these are not suggested stages into which to split your expeditions. If you ended your walk directly on the county boundaries, you would always find yourself in the middle of nowhere. Each county chapter is subdivided into shorter sections, listed on the contents page and in the route summary table (Appendix A), to help you determine your own itinerary. Appendix C gives information on facilities along the way so that you can choose where to overnight and stop for refreshments.

By way of facilitating a return to urban civilisation, a 15-mile link has been added from the end of the official Severn Way at Severn Beach into the bustling heart of the city of Bristol. This is included at the end of the Gloucestershire chapter, although it passes into the County of Bristol.

Each section of the route is accompanied by an extract from the Ordnance Survey 1:50,000 map with overlays showing the route described. An information box gives the start and finish point, distance (km/miles) and (where applicable) ascent and descent. Within the route description text, points of interest are included to help you make the most of your visits to places along the way.

The rising path into the upper Hafren Forest

The Severn Way

Distance views across the Plynlimon moorland to Pen Plynlimon

To undertake a walk that has its starting point high on the peaty uplands of Plynlimon means adding to the journey before it begins because of the need to first trek to the source of the river.

The nearest point to the source accessible by road is the picnic area and car park at Rhyd-y-benwch in Hafren Forest. Later in this section, a variant start is given from Eisteddfa Gurig on the A44 between Ponterwyd and Llangurig in the Wye valley, which takes in the summit of Plynlimon Fawr (Pumlumon Fawr). This route is not part of the Severn Way; it is not waymarked, and should not be considered in poor visibility, although there are fences across the summit plateau. It makes an interesting variant start for those who don't relish ending Day 1 exactly where it started...in Llanidloes.

Undoubtedly, the greatest charm of the Plynlimon massif is a geographical one, for the mountain's peaty folds give rise to several watercourses, including three significant rivers, the Wye, the Severn and the Rheidol, and two others, the Ystwyth and the Clywedog. Each explores enchanting countryside on its journey to the sea, and the greatest of these is the Severn, the longest river in Britain.

The wild summits, rolling moorlands and deep valleys that flank Plynlimon have for centuries acted as a redoubtable barrier, making this one of the least-known parts of Wales. Today, it is this remote and peaceful atmosphere that is the area's greatest asset, and the great river that flows from it provides an unparalleled opportunity to enjoy a fascinating source-to-sea walk.

STAGE 1
Rhyd-y-benwch to the source

Start	Rhyd-y-benwch
Finish	The source
Distance	5.5km (3½ miles)
Ascent	340m (1120ft)
Descent	65m (210ft)

With the exception of the final 1km (½ mile), the walk from Rhyd-y-benwch to the source of the river and back is almost entirely within the confines of the Hafren Forest; perfect on a fine day, not so good in the rain.

Be aware that the trails through Hafren Forest are permissive and not public rights of way. Motorsport events and harvesting operations in the forest may affect the use of certain trails. Phone 0300 068 0300 or visit www.ccw.gov.uk for more details.

From Rhyd-y-benwch, head beneath a wooden arch and turn down a surfaced path that leads swiftly to the Severn, at this point a well-defined stream with occasional flashes of white to hallmark the force of the river both above and below this point. On reaching the river, continue

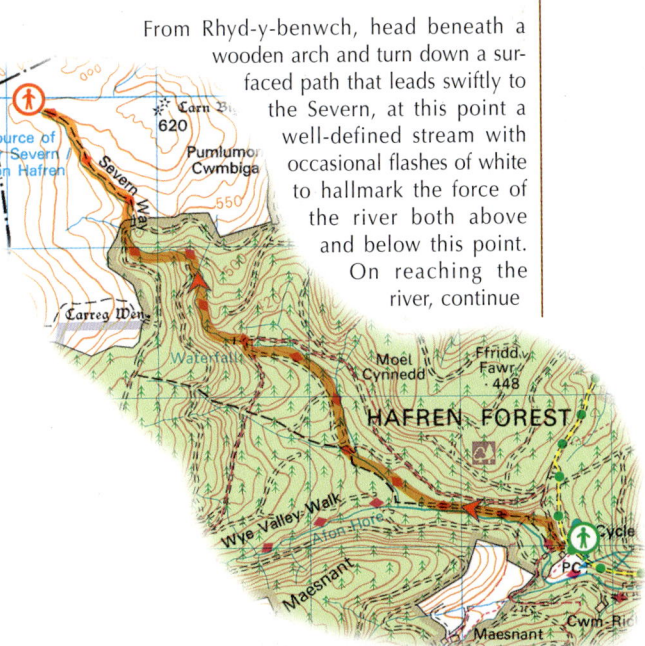

along a raised boardwalk. A waterfall of no great stature towards the end of the boardwalk was used by generations of shepherds for washing sheep. Here, rise onto a pleasant forest path that soon reaches a flume station used to measure the river discharge of the Severn. Beyond, an on-going path runs parallel to the river, and at a waymark, shortly after a picnic shelter and at the confluence of the Severn and the **Afon Hore**, turns into the mature forest and soon reaches a footbridge.

HAFREN FOREST

Heathered pathway near the top of Hafren Forest

The 2842ha (7022 acres) of Hafren Forest are located in the south-west corner of the historic county of Montgomeryshire (now part of Powys), among the rolling hills of the mid-Wales Cambrian Mountain range. The ancient county is named after Roger de Montgomerie, the 1st Earl of Shrewsbury and one of William the Conqueror's main counsellors. The topography of the forest covers gently rounded hill tops and steep valley sides, dissected by many kilometres of streams and rivers. Surrounding the forest are thousands of acres of grassland, traditionally used for grazing sheep. A large proportion of the forest borders the Plynlimon Site of Special Scientific Interest (SSSI).

Development of the forest aims to provide an attractive place for people to enjoy, including walkers, cyclists and motorsport enthusiasts, and it is especially encouraging to see that the forest's rich wildlife, historical features

STAGE 1 – RHYD-Y-BENWCH TO THE SOURCE

and water quality are being managed sensitively, consistent with the need to supply a range of sustainable timber products.

The ancient Celts saw this region as magical, and this certainly holds true in ecological terms, with waterside forests being rich and valuable habitats – a home to organisms of woodland and water. Riparian woodlands, as they are known, are those on the banks of natural bodies of water and particularly rivers.

Rivers are the lifeblood of the forest ecosystems, and their health is crucial to the health of the forest as a whole. The physical presence of trees on the river's edge, such as the deep-rooted alder (*Alnus glutinosa*), helps to prevent the banks from eroding. Riparian zones are important sources and storage sites for nutrients and energy, since trees naturally alter the chemical balance of the water by taking up minerals from the soil and releasing them into the water, so improving the biological health of the river. The riparian corridors enhance connectivity, creating links within and between forest patches, and in doing so provide routes along which animals can disperse, as well as certain plant seeds, which may be carried by mammals, birds, or even water.

Hafren is also an important location for research into climate change, and water and air quality. The Centre of Ecology and Hydrology has carried out work in this area for over 40 years. At a commercial level Hafren produces 26,300 tonnes of timber annually. This is approved felling and independently assessed by the FSC (Forestry Stewardship Council) as sustainably produced certificated timber.

After the footbridge, the path continues pleasantly along the true right bank of the river, before crossing it again near another flume station, just after which bear right, following a route waymarked by blue-and-white banded poles. The path climbs steadily, eventually intercepting a broad forest trail. Bear right briefly, passing the **Blaen Hafren Falls**, and then swing left once more climbing into forest.

Approaching the top of the forest, clear-felling is evident, but this serves only to open up the vistas of distant hills in the heart of Powys. Here, a seat for one to the right of the path offers a brief respite and a fabulous retrospective view eastwards. The path continues to climb steadily and, near the top edge of the forest, joins another broad trail. Turn right on this, once more briefly, and then leave it for a constructed path that leads up to the source of the Severn.

The Way passes through a beautiful landscape of peaty mounds and heather banks that in September especially are a joy. Climbing very gradually, the path becomes paved and leads directly to a large post placed in marshy ground at the official **source of the River Severn**, although it is clear that there is flowing water a little higher still.

There is no need now to do anything other than to turn about and start the descent. But on a clear day there is much merit in following the flagged path a little further, to the **Ceredigion and Powys county boundary**, and crossing a stile in a fence to walk up to a boundary stone and cairn with an outstanding view of the distant Tarren Hills above Machynlleth, the Cadair Idris massif and the Arans – Fawddwy and Benllyn. This modest extension is well worth the effort and the nearby lake something of a pleasant surprise. Nearby, a fence runs up onto Pumlumon Arwystli, beyond which rises the peak of Plynlimon Fawr, at 752m (2467ft) the highest point of the landscape hereabouts.

Cairn above the Ceredigion and Powys county boundary; it's all downhill from here

VARIANT START: EISTEDDFA GURIG TO THE SOURCE VIA PLYNLIMON

Start	Eisteddfa Gurig
Finish	The source
Distance	8.9km (5½ miles)
Ascent	420m (1380ft)
Descent	250m (815ft)

Not everyone will want to make the ascent from Rhyd-y-benwch; there is a certain inevitability and repetitiveness about it. But this can be avoided by starting at Eisteddfa Gurig, to the south of Plynlimon Fawr, and taking a perfectly valid, if a little more difficult, route to the source. The route, straightforward in itself, climbs first to Plynlimon, the highest summit of the massif that spawns the Severn, and arguably more than justified on that account. Instead of starting at the source of the river, you start at the top of the mountain that hosts the course.

This variant start is not part of the Severn Way, and is not waymarked at any point. It is straightforward as far as the summit of Plynlimon Fawr. But the onward stretch from there, over Pen Punlumon Arwystli and along the county boundary to the source of the Severn is mostly trackless, extremely demanding and boggy, and should be contemplated only by strong and experienced walkers/navigators and, preferably, in clear weather conditions. Nor is it advised after prolonged periods of rain.

The variant begins at a private parking area adjoining the farmhouse at Eisteddfa Gurig. From the parking area cross a surfaced yard in a north-westerly direction to a gate, and then pass between farm buildings and the garden wall of the farmhouse before turning right past dog kennels and left to join a track. Turn right here and follow the track to a gate with a sign 'All Walks'. Beyond the gate, the track swings round to follow the course of the Afon Tarennig, and climbs steadily. After another gate, the track levels and starts to descend briefly, climbing again towards **old mine workings**. Here, at a waymark post, branch left onto a stony path that suddenly comes to an end.

THE SEVERN WAY

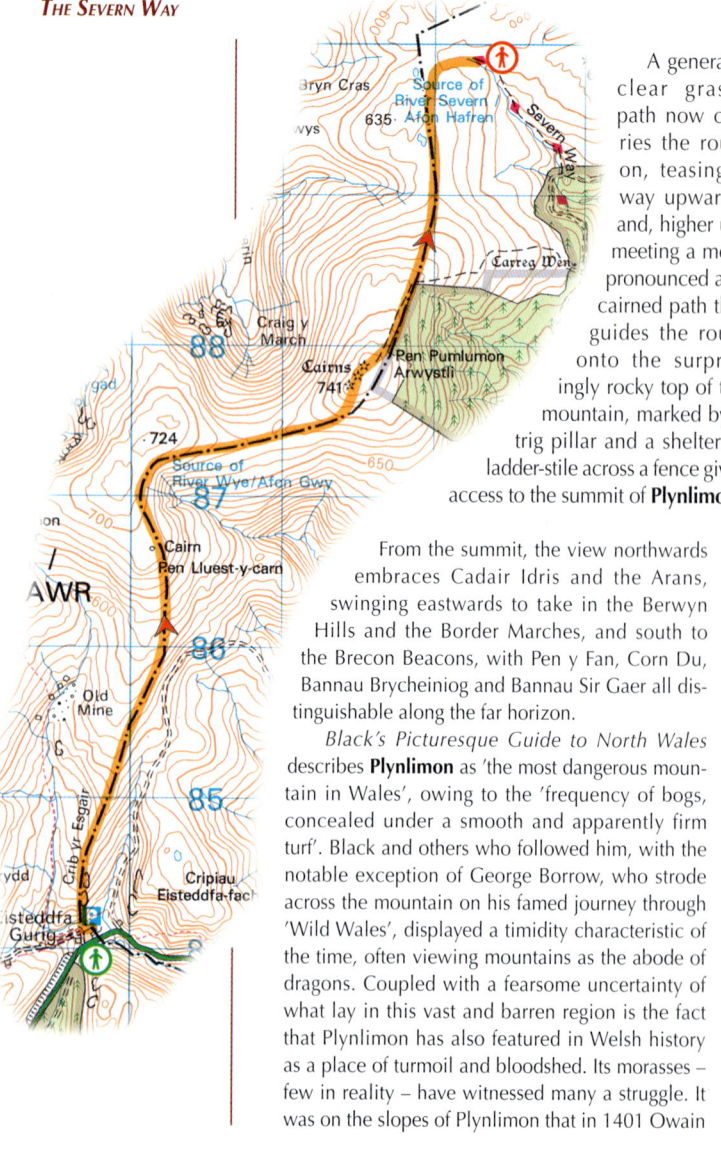

A generally clear grassy path now carries the route on, teasing a way upwards, and, higher up, meeting a more pronounced and cairned path that guides the route onto the surprisingly rocky top of the mountain, marked by a trig pillar and a shelter. A ladder-stile across a fence gives access to the summit of **Plynlimon**.

From the summit, the view northwards embraces Cadair Idris and the Arans, swinging eastwards to take in the Berwyn Hills and the Border Marches, and south to the Brecon Beacons, with Pen y Fan, Corn Du, Bannau Brycheiniog and Bannau Sir Gaer all distinguishable along the far horizon.

Black's Picturesque Guide to North Wales describes **Plynlimon** as 'the most dangerous mountain in Wales', owing to the 'frequency of bogs, concealed under a smooth and apparently firm turf'. Black and others who followed him, with the notable exception of George Borrow, who strode across the mountain on his famed journey through 'Wild Wales', displayed a timidity characteristic of the time, often viewing mountains as the abode of dragons. Coupled with a fearsome uncertainty of what lay in this vast and barren region is the fact that Plynlimon has also featured in Welsh history as a place of turmoil and bloodshed. Its morasses – few in reality – have witnessed many a struggle. It was on the slopes of Plynlimon that in 1401 Owain

STAGE 2 – SOURCE OF THE SEVERN TO LLANIDLOES

The 'official' source of the Severn

Glyndwr gave renewed impetus to his rebellion against the English with an important military victory, before going on to sack Montgomery, burn Welshpool and destroy the abbey of Cwmhir.

▶ The continuation to the source of the Severn sets off by following the ridge fenceline in a west-north-westerly direction to cross **Pen Pumlumon Arwystli** – site of Bronze Age stone cairns – and then descending beside a fence to intercept the path rising from the source of the Severn. Here, by a stile, turn right, and follow a paved route through low peat mounds of bracken and heather to the **source**.

Paddy Dillon's guide to Glyndwr's Way follows the National Trail named in his honour which loops from Knighton to Welshpool, via this historic site.

STAGE 2
Source of the Severn to Llanidloes

Start	Source of the Severn
Finish	Llanidloes
Distance	18.3km (11½ miles)
Ascent	295m (960ft)
Descent	730m (2390ft)

THE SEVERN WAY

As the end of the Severn Way approaches and you reflect on the days gone by, the stretch up to the source of the river will hold special appeal. Not because it was the start, nor because it was the highest point and among mountains, but because there is a refined sense of wildness that is not present once the valley takes hold. There are lovely views up here, especially so for those that make it a little way beyond the source, across the watershed and up to the minor hill that lies beyond. But there is also an inner satisfaction in being at the birth of such a great river, the bringer of life on so many levels.

Once back at Rhyd-y-benwch, virtually the entire stretch to Llanidloes follows a country lane, which makes this first day a little less demanding than it might otherwise be. The upper section of the forest has been clear-felled, and brings the wonderful openness of the tops sooner than of old. This is a peaty, heathery landscape that in spite of the hardships it can pose for walkers – although not those on the mostly paved Severn Way – is an invigorating and inspiring place.

Start the journey by leaving the source of the Severn and heading back to **Hafren Forest** following a paved path that leads down alongside the infant river, now no more than a bustling stream, a brash youngster and a far cry from the mature river it is to become. Gradually, the path descends to intercept a broad forest track. Here, turn right briefly, crossing the Severn, and then immediately bear left onto a descending path on the

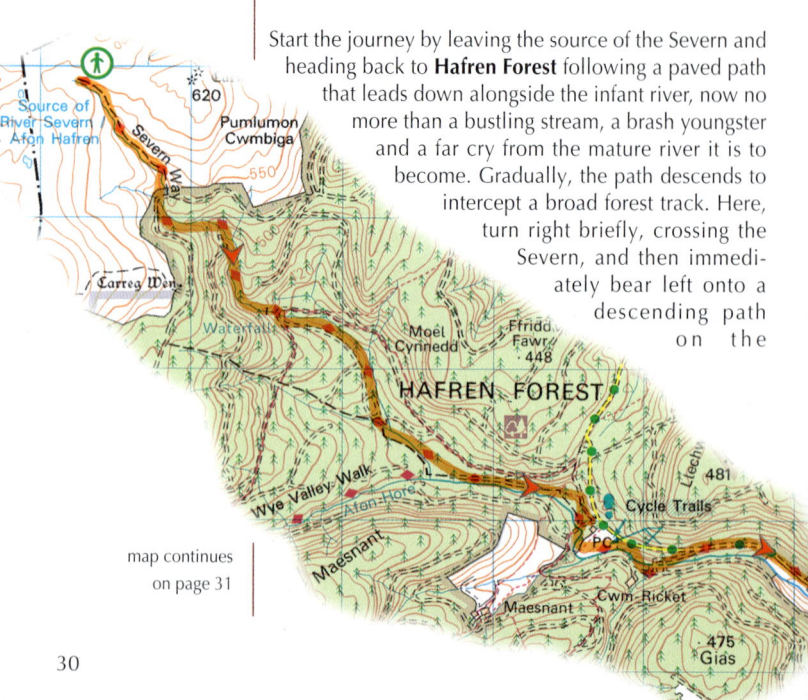

map continues on page 31

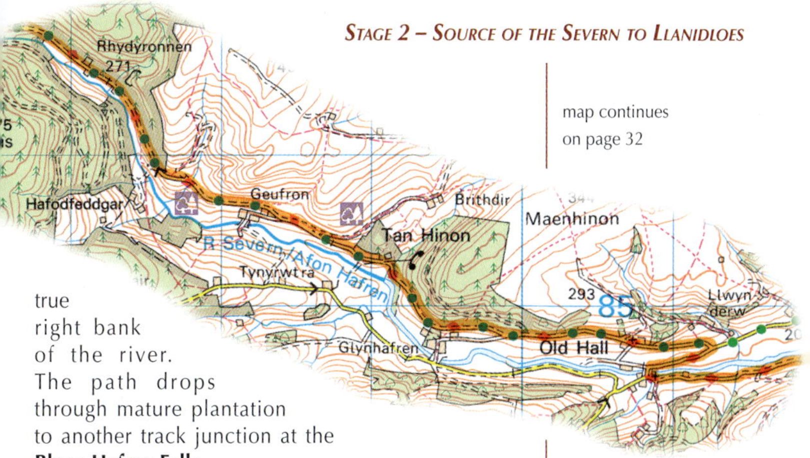

STAGE 2 – SOURCE OF THE SEVERN TO LLANIDLOES

map continues on page 32

true
right bank
of the river.
The path drops
through mature plantation
to another track junction at the
Blaen Hafren Falls.

Turn right briefly, but within a few strides bear left onto a descending path back towards the river. The way down follows a clear track and re-crosses the river, before continuing through a break in the forest through which the river now flows. Part way down this, cross the river by a footbridge – do not take the Wye Valley Walk. Continue down to a clear bend, near the confluence with the **Afon**

The final walk out to Rhyd-y-benwch

THE SEVERN WAY

Hore, and turn left to follow a broad riverside path that eventually feeds onto a section of boardwalk.

As you approach Rhyd-y-benwch and pass a ford (just below a path leading up to the car park), branch right on a riverside gravel path. Pass a footbridge and immediately climb left to the edge of the field, soon reaching a picnic area overlooking the river. Continue along the path, which gives onto another stretch of boardwalk and then into forest. After leaving the trees, cross a bridge to the right bank, and follow a broad track to an attractive spot known as Severn-break-its-neck, where the falls are rather special. Cross a bridge here, and climb on the other side to a broad track. Turn right to reach the valley road. Now road walking leads all the way to Llanidloes.

Once the forest is left behind, so the valley opens up ahead, a lush landscape of farmland and grassy hillsides patterned by hedgerows and dotted with farm buildings. The road leads past Hen Neuadd (**Old Hall**), and on to a junction with a road arriving from the right. Turn right here and descend to cross the Severn, then immediately turn left onto a narrow lane. Pass the old chapel at Glanhafren, and keep following this relatively quiet back road for 4km (2½ miles) to a T-junction. Turn left and soon cross the Severn again at Felindre Bridge.

The lane now leads up to the valley road. Turn right and walk towards **Llanidloes**. On reaching the town, turn right over Short Bridge and walk up to the market hall in the centre of town.

STAGE 3
Llanidloes to Caersws

Start	Llanidloes
Finish	Caersws
Distance	15.5km (9¾ miles)
Ascent	330m (1080ft)
Descent	375m (1230ft)

Precious little will be seen of the Severn in this traverse to Caersws. But, by way of compensation, the landscape is one of great beauty, a delightful undulating assortment of grassy and wooded hillsides, peppered with isolated farms and small communities over which buzzard, raven and red kite put on aerial displays, and along which the pathways are enlivened by ancient hedgerows of hazel, blackthorn and gorse.

The Way enters Llanidloes over the so-called Short Bridge. To reach the town centre, follow the road to its end, to the beautiful market hall. Anyone visiting the centre should then either backtrack to Short Bridge to continue the walk, or simply head down the High Street to Long Bridge, resuming the route there.

The strict continuation of the Severn Way, however, turns left after Short Bridge into Penygraig Street, and passes a row of cottages to arrive at the church of St Idloes, which stands on a riverside site said to have been chosen by the saint himself.

map continues on page 37

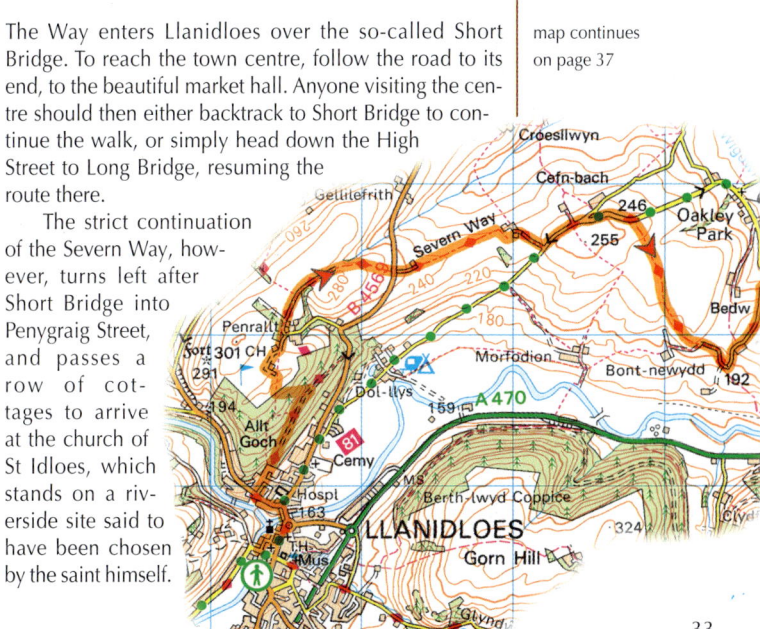

LLANIDLOES

The old market hall

Llanidloes is at the heart of the ancient medieval kingdom of Arwystli, and is a town rich in history. Tumuli and cairns on the summits of the hills above bear witness to human habitation from at least Bronze Age times, while the Romans built roads and mined for lead here during the first centuries of the new age.

The origins of Llanidloes date from the seventh century, when the Celtic Saint Idloes laid the foundations of a church on land overlooking the Severn. The town began to expand following the Norman Conquest in the 11th century, when a motte and bailey castle was constructed at the western end of the town, on the site where the Mount Inn now stands.

In 1280, Llanidloes obtained its first Charter, granted by Edward I, and this was followed in 1344 by a Charter making the town a self-governing borough; a status that was retained until the local government re-organisation of 1974. The layout of wide streets in the shape of a cross that form the heart of the town originated at this time; the Old Market Hall, the only half-timbered hall of its kind in Wales still in its original position, was constructed on the centre of the cross between 1612 and 1622, although it is known that there was an earlier market hall at this spot.

Llanidloes, always an industrious centre, gained renown in the 16th century for the quality of its wool, and during the 18th and 19th centuries its flannel. But perhaps the most striking incident in the town's long history arose during a depression in the flannel industry in the 1830s linked with an attendant movement for political reform. Llanidloes was by no means unique in having a Chartist movement, but in the spring of 1839, a riot effectively overthrew the constituted authority of the town for five days, until troops could be mustered to restore order. Llanidloes remained an occupied town for a whole year, while a number of trials saw the harsh sentences of transportation and imprisonment imposed on more than a hundred people. During the mid-19th century, the area developed as a lead smelting industry, processing ore mined from the local Van and Bryn Tail lead mines. At this time the population of Llanidloes rose to almost 5000, an explosion that left its mark on the town, not least in the number of public houses and chapels of conflicting denomination. Indeed, the present Town Hall was first built as a temperance hotel, an enterprise that failed here as it failed pretty well everywhere else in Britain.

Pass to the left of the church and walk down a bendy path to the riverside, where the river for the moment flows sedately, and follow this until deflected out to the edge of Long Bridge, spanning the river. Turn left, crossing the bridge, and then turn left into Westgate Street.

Walk up the street until, just after the second turning into Tan yr Allt, a footpath on the right leaves the road heading into the **Allt Goch** woodlands.

In the Allt Goch woodland

> In the 17th century, the lands at Allt Goch and Pen yr Allt, were unenclosed common land, but under the provisions of the Enclosure Acts of the 19th century they were divided among various landowners. The **Allt Goch woodlands** are now managed by Llanidloes Town Council, and the area was replanted in the 1990s with a mixture of broadleaved trees, notably oak, sycamore, beech, birch, holly and hazel along with Scots pine and Douglas fir.

Shortly after entering the woodland the path divides at a waymark. Here, keep right on a gently ascending path which later joins a wider forest trail. Keep forward, ignoring all branching paths until another waymark (Severn Way) is reached at SN 956 856, just as the trail levels. Turn sharply left onto a narrow path, once more rising through the woodland before gradually descending as it skirts the edge of a golf course.

Eventually, the path pops out onto the golf course. Keep to the right and walk up towards the **club house** and there turn right onto an access lane. Walk for about 100m, and then turn left at a waymark to **Penrallt Farm**. A track leads up past the farm, and through the right-hand one of three metal gates giving onto a broad track. Follow this track, which later passes through a field gate, and then runs alongside a fence. When the fence changes direction, keep forward along a grassy track to a gate, here departing Glyndwr's Way. Beyond, the route descends into a hedgeway, a clearly defined path flanked by gorse, blackthorn and hazel, which leads down to intercept a road.

Cross the road, and keep on in the same direction, entering a broad gravel track, again flanked by hedgerows, signposted for Caersws. The track leads down to an open arable field. Follow the right-hand field boundary. On the far side of the field, the track is once again enclosed and leads to Cefnmawr Farm. There turn right around the farm boundary to reach its access lane.

Press on along the access track to meet a lane, and there turn left. When the lane forks, keep right, and

STAGE 3 – LLANIDLOES TO CAERSWS

follow the lane for a short distance until, at SN 978 867, the Way takes a broad track descending on the right. At the bottom of the track, go through the right-hand one of two field gates, and continue climbing gently along the edge of a pasture with a hedgerow and fence on the left. Follow the field boundary as it descends to a gate into an enclosed neck of land. Through the gate turn right and keep to the left-hand side following a hedgerow, with the Severn only now coming back into view, the first glimpse since leaving Llanidloes.

At the end of the hedgerow, cross the middle of a sloping pasture to another gate, and then continue once more with a hedge of gorse and hawthorn on the left and **Bontnewydd Farm** down on the right. The Way continues as a broad grassy track and leads down to a farm access track. Turn left and follow the track down. At the bottom, turn left onto an ascending surfaced lane, climbing to pass Pentre Farm. Follow the lane down and cross a road, and then keep on in the same direction.

Stay with the lane, which finally climbs up to **Wigdwr Farm**, and then, as the road swings sharply to the left, leave it on the

map continues on page 39

bend by going forward through a gate on the right into an ascending track between hedgerows. The track presses on through a dip and then rises to a gate, where it turns left into a field. At this point, go through a field gate and forward along a broad grassy track that begins with a dilapidated corrugated iron shed (SN 998 869). Keep on through a single gate, and a short way further on enter a holloway, an old sunken track flanked by hazel, that gives into the corner of a sloping pasture. The path leads up to join a lane. Turn left, and a few strides later turn right, continuing on a surfaced lane.

When the road surface ends, keep ahead on a bridleway between hedgerows. Follow the track until it swings right up towards a stand of woodland where the track continues along the right-hand edge of the woodland. But here, on reaching a gate, turn left to walk with the woodland to the right – a dead oak mid-field is a useful indicator of the correct field location. Follow the woodland boundary to cross a track and descend to a field gate beyond which a grassy track rises through the middle of a pasture, bearing left to a waymark from where the route

Tidy farmland pastures

STAGE 3 – LLANIDLOES TO CAERSWS

continues diagonally up-field to then run along another woodland boundary as an old sunken track.

In the corner of the field, enter a woodland path that feeds into the bottom edge of sloping pasture and continues parallel with a hedgerow. When the path comes out to meet a broader track, turn left towards a radio mast, and then walk with the track until it swings to the right. There, leave it on the apex, to go down a grassy track, with the route now starting to descend, and once more follow a woodland edge down to a gate. Walk down to the bottom of Waen Lane, to a T-junction, and there turn right. When the road swings to the right, leave it branching left towards Lower Gwerneirin Farm.

Stay on the lane as it passes Llandinam Water Treatment Works, and go past the farm and then, beyond a couple of gates, the track forks. Take the left-hand track briefly, as far as a waymark.

The Severn Way

Branch right at the waymark to follow a terraced grassy path, with the river once more in view. The route undulates forward pleasantly across lightly wooded pastures and bracken-clad slopes. The path feeds into a gravel track that runs out to **Carnedd Farm**, and on to cross reed-fringed **Afon Cerist**. Turn right along a lane and walk as far as a T-junction with the **B4569**, where the route turns right, immediately crossing the **Afon Carno**, to walk into **Caersws**.

Having crossed the railway, take the first road on the right and follow this round to meet and cross the main road through the village.

CAERSWS

Caersws village hall

The village of Caersws is an important centre for the upper Severn valley. Although unremarkable in itself, it enjoys a lovely setting. The village – or is it a small town? – owes its existence to two periods of development, the first being the establishment of a Roman fort here around AD70, principally to exploit Plynlimon's lead reserves. The earthworks of the fort are still discernible near the railway station. The second was the coming of the railways in the 1860s. The railways, as elsewhere in Britain, led to a booming industry with hundreds of people employed by the railways directly, and with many more working in the industries that benefited from the communication links with the rest of Britain. Construction of the Newtown to Machynlleth line began in 1857 and was completed in 1862, and became part of the Cambrian railway network in 1864. It was in that year that Caersws Station opened.

The next railway to serve the village was the Van Line, constructed by the Van Railway Company in 1871 to serve the Van Lead and Barites Mine near Llanidloes. The general manager and superintendent of the line was John Ceiriog Hughes (1832–1887), who lived at a cottage nearby. He was a lyric poet who wrote the Oriau series of poems and many well-known songs that are still performed at eisteddfods (festivals of literature, music and performance) to this day. He won prizes at the London, Llangollen and Merthyr eisteddfods. The name Caersws means 'Fort of Sws'. The prefix is the Welsh *Caer*, meaning fort, and it has been suggested that Swswen was an ancient queen from Roman times.

STAGE 4
Caersws to Newtown

Start	Caersws
Finish	Newtown
Distance	13.5km (8½ miles)
Ascent	325m (1070ft)
Descent	345m (1130ft)

As with the section from Llanidloes to Caersws, very little is seen of the Severn river during this crossing to Newtown; it might almost not exist, being seen only at the start and at the very end. But the undulating landscape through which the Way teases a route is rambling of the very best quality, excellent walking, with changing views almost by the stride, nooks and crannies in profusion, and views of distant hills that are constantly changing as the route casts about to find what in the event is a very satisfying way to Newtown.

In Caersws, go along the road for Aberhafesp, past the Red Lion pub, the attractive village hall (1902) and the Buck Hotel. Continue past **Plas Mallwyn**, and make the most of a brief glimpse of the river on the right. A short way further on, leave the road as it bends to the left by turning onto a broad gravel track on the right (for Newtown).

THE SEVERN WAY

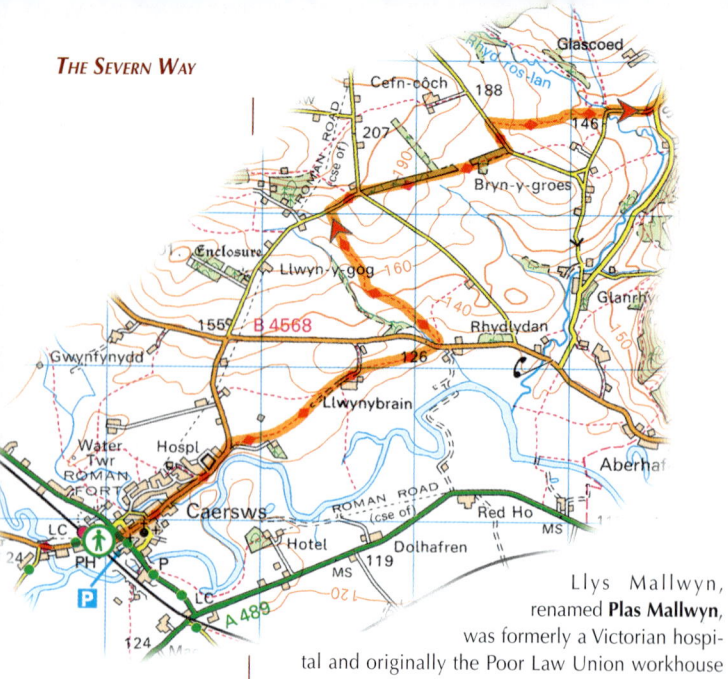

map continues on page 45

Llys Mallwyn, renamed **Plas Mallwyn**, was formerly a Victorian hospital and originally the Poor Law Union workhouse for Newtown and Llanidloes District.

A short way along the track lie the remains of **Caersws I**, the earlier of the two Roman forts at Caersws constructed and occupied during the first century. This was a short-lived fort, and today only slight earthworks remain.

Within 40m of leaving the road, bear left through a metal gate to pursue a narrow grassy path across a pasture, then continue across more fields to a gate in a corner by a single oak tree from which the track runs alongside a fence towards **Llwyn-y-brain Farm**. Follow a gated and waymarked route around the farm to its access track. Do not use the access; instead stay within rough pasture to a single gate where the access can now be crossed. A large pasture (trackless, as many of the fields in this section will be) ensues; traverse it to a field gate, and keep on across the next field using an old oak as a guide down to a gate into a lane.

Llys Mallwyn, renamed Plas Mallwyn, Caersws

Cross the lane diagonally right to a signpost, and then, through a metal gate, turn sharply left to walk beside a ditch to a field gate in a corner. Beyond the gate, walk up beside a hedgerow on the right. On the far side of the field, go through the middle one of three gates, and turn right to a signpost and from it head out across the lower part of a sloping pasture to a field gate at a corner. From here, go forward with a hawthorn hedge to the right to meet a lane.

Turn right and walk up the lane to a junction on the right, and there cross a stile into a shaded path through trees. At the end of the path, cross two stiles into a large open pasture and keep forward along the headland. On the left, and arguably the original right of way, is a sunken track, now an intermittent watercourse. At the bottom of the field cross a stile and bridge, and then keep on in the same direction, once more within the shelter of trees.

The track leads out to a road. Turn left and follow it for about 200m, as far as a gate and signpost on the right. Through the gate, head half-right across the centre of a large field. In the far corner, cross a footbridge, and go through a gate, and then from a nearby signpost strike across the middle of the next field towards a mid-field waymark. Press on down to a gate at the bottom of the field.

Just through the gate on the left is a memorial to nine airmen of the **Heavy Conversion Unit Faldingworth** who died when their aircraft crashed on Glascoed and Cwm farms in January 1944.

From the gate bear right below power lines, and walk out to a gate into a road. Turn left across a bridge, and follow the road. Cross the Caersws road and keep on in the same direction following the lane to turn into a signposted track on the right, at SO 073 951. Walk a short distance up as far as a gate, and then climb steeply left alongside a hedgerow. From the high point, drop below power lines to a footbridge in a wooded dell. After a gate just beyond the footbridge, go forward across rough pasture to a waymark, and on to enter woodland, climbing on a broad track. On leaving the trees, follow a broad green track, slightly to the left, and still climbing. After a short climb, the track swings right alongside a fence. Then as the track swings left, break off and go through a gate and climb to a waymark at the foot of a low grassy hill.

Keep to the left of the hill, but then climb to bear right across its shoulder, and head up to a waymarked stile in a hedgerow and fence. Over this, head downfield to the bottom corner, to join another lane. Turn right and when the lane swings to the right, leave it on the apex for another, narrower lane. When this also swings sharply to the right, at a signpost, keep to the left, into the edge of woodland, and climb steadily to a field gate beyond which a broad grassy track runs on alongside a fence.

As you cross the high point, so Fachwen Pool comes into view below, set amid gently rolling hills. Descend a clear track as far as a waymark, and then drop steeply to a gate at the edge of woodland, close by a small pond. Cross the streambed issuing from the pond, and in the next field keep forward alongside a hedgerow and shortly arrive at **Fachwen Pool**, popular with anglers and wildfowl alike.

Past the pool, go left along a field edge to a stile. Carry on slightly above the pool, and walk out to meet a lane. Continue down the lane to a signpost at SO 084 930, and here turn left, descending to reach a graveyard.

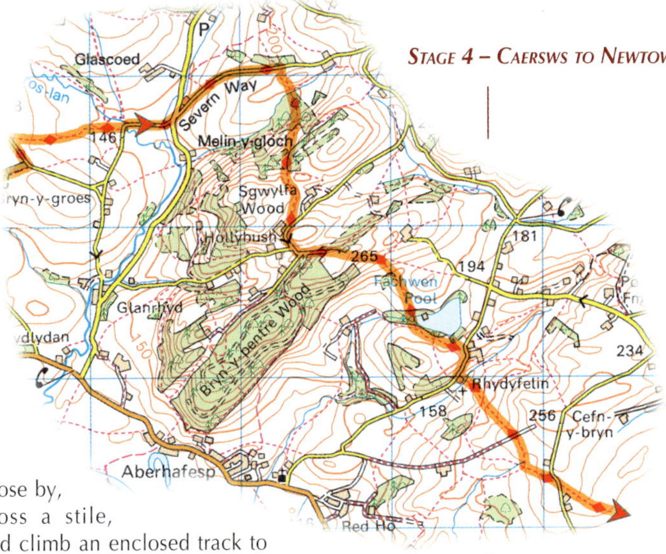

STAGE 4 – CAERSWS TO NEWTOWN

Close by, cross a stile, and climb an enclosed track to reach a large domed pasture. Strike upfield, roughly aiming for two leaning conifers on the skyline, but then closing in on a step-stile in a field corner. A little further climbing ensues, to a gate, and then across the top edge of a field. More undulating pastures lie ahead, before the Way crosses a road and starts the

map continues on page 46

Fachwen Pool

descent to Newtown, bearing half-right from the road across a pasture to a gate.

From the high point, gradually now descend more pastures, all linked by gates, walking forward into a lush landscape of hedgerowed field and woodland coppices.

Eventually, the descending path feeds into the top edge of woodland, through which a broad track drops to a gate into a sunken track, and eventually comes out onto an estate road. Cross this, and continue descending to meet a road on the edge of **Newtown**. Turn left and walk as far as the entrance to Dolerw Park on the right. Go into the park, soon passing the Gorsedd stone circle, which marks the site of the Newtown eisteddfod, held in 1965. Follow the parkland path to a suspension bridge crossing the Severn, and then turn left along a riverside path that leads around Newtown.

NEWTOWN

The Severn at Newtown

Built on the banks of the Severn, in one of the most visually compelling areas in Wales, Newtown's small-town charm is underpinned by a thriving business community. Residents and visitors alike enjoy excellent shopping, first-class theatres, museums and art galleries, and all in the crucible of the upper Severn valley.

The town (Drenewydd in Welsh) has an ancient pedigree – scratch the surface here and it bleeds history – and was a market town as long ago as the 13th century, although the local council's website (www.newtown.org.uk) suggests that it came into being only in 1321. It acquired its name in 1279, when Roger Mortimer was granted a market charter by Edward I, who also commissioned him to build a centre, on lands seized from Llywelyn ap Gruffudd, Prince of Wales, for a hamlet previously known as Llanfair-yng-Nghedewain. The two names – the latter abbreviated to Llanfair Cedewain – were used interchangeably until 1832. The town grew in the 18th and 19th centuries around the textile and flannel industries, stimulated by the completion of the Montgomery Canal. Today, Newtown is the largest town in mid-Wales, with numerous shops, pubs, cafés and restaurants.

Within the ruins of the church of St Mary is the resting place of the Pryce family, founders of Pryce Jones, the world's first ever mail order company. But Newtown is arguably better known as the birthplace of Robert Owen, advocate of trades unions and the founder of the Co-operative movement, who set new standards in business by providing workers with better living and working conditions, and went on to establish model communities in Scotland and America. In an online poll conducted in 2003 by Culturenet Cymru to determine '100 Welsh Heroes' and showcase the extraordinary talents of Welsh men and women through the ages, Robert Owen was voted ninth overall and first in the 'Thinkers' category.

STAGE 5
Newtown to Welshpool

Start	Newtown
Finish	Welshpool
Distance	23km (14½ miles)
Ascent	120m (400ft)
Descent	150m (500ft)

The long stretch from Newtown to Welshpool is not as arduous as it might seem. It follows the Montgomery Canal for much of the journey, and that alone foretells easy walking. And so it is. But it is easy walking endowed with amazing landscapes of soft-moulded hills, lush farmland and riparian loveliness that should be treated with respect, and, insofar as time allows, dawdled over. Make a whole day of this stretch, take time to enjoy the wildlife – at certain times of year, protective swans may prove to be an obstacle to progress – and make the most of what is the first day of gentle walking.

From the bridge exiting Dolerw Park, the Severn Way turns immediately left by the river (signed for Abermule), and follows a surfaced path beneath a road bridge. Keep on below another pedestrian footbridge, known locally as Ha'penny Bridge, which until recently was regularly swept away by the winter floods. Go past the bridge, and, at the end of a wall, double back to cross the bridge. On the other side, turn immediately right and walk along the top of an embankment, and shortly descend to join a riverside path and pass beneath another road bridge.

STAGE 5 – NEWTOWN TO WELSHPOOL

After the bridge, you can return to the embankment for a slightly elevated view of the nearby river. This higher and a lower, surfaced path converge at a gate. Continue past the Old Pump House, and then press on through riverside broadleaved woodland. The path passes around **sewage treatment works**, and soon reaches the entrance to the Pwll Penarth Nature Reserve. Very soon a dry section of the **Montgomery Canal** is reached.

Three different companies built the cross-border **Montgomery Canal**, over a period of 30 years, during which time it was opened in sections between 1796 and 1819. In 1821, it finally reached Newtown, about 56km (35 miles) from its junction with the Llangollen Canal at Frankton. Limestone and coal were the main items of trade going towards Newtown, while the main trade in the opposite direction was timber, grain and dairy produce.

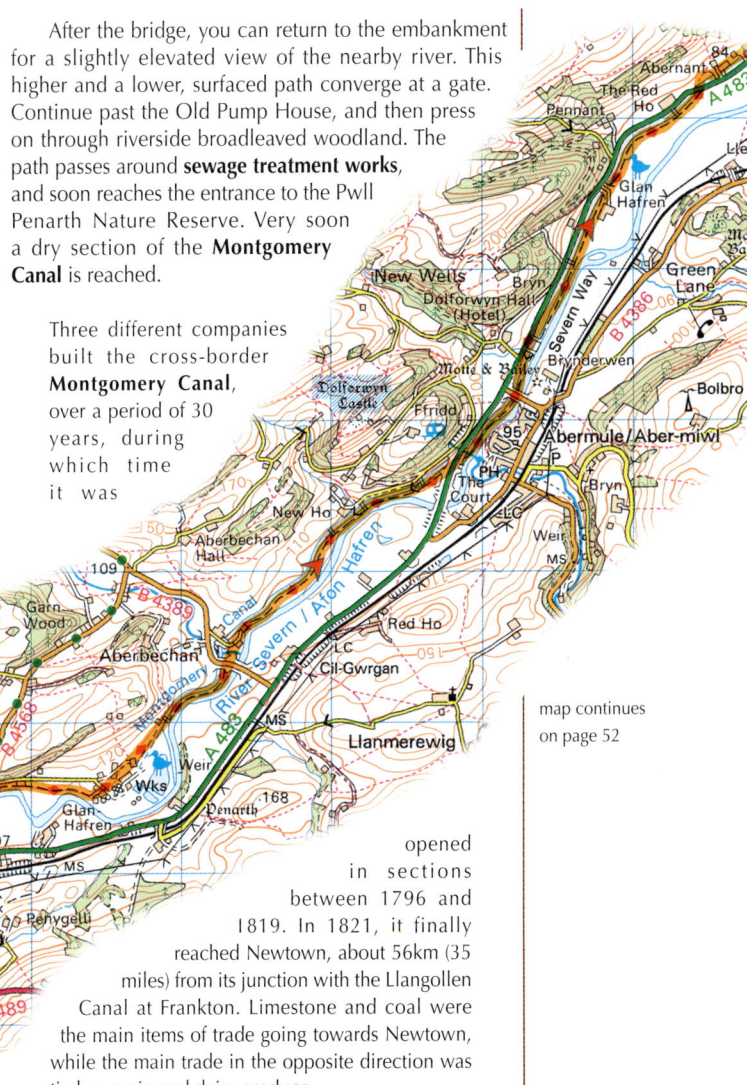

map continues on page 52

'The second iron bridge to be built in Montgomeryshire'

By 1850, the canal had become part of the network of the Shropshire Union Railway and Canal Company. It was unofficially abandoned in 1935 (officially 1944), following a breach at Frankton, and has subsequently developed into a wonderful reedy wildlife paradise.

The onward route past the Pwll Penarth Nature Reserve flanks the old towpath alongside the canal bed, which is dry at this point. On reaching Freestone Loch, the canal is filled with water.

With little need for description, since it is well way-marked, the Severn Way now follows the canal towpath all the way to Welshpool. When the route confronts the **A483** not far from Abermule, it doubles back to pass beneath the road, beyond which the canal and the river reappear. A little further on, a fine metal bridge (1853) calls for a pause, the magnificent span of the second iron bridge to be built in Montgomeryshire, replacing the original Brynderwen Bridge (300m downriver), which was built of wood, and had been washed away by floods. Close by stands Dolforwyn Castle.

Dolforwyn means 'the maid's meadow'. The **castle** was built by Llywelyn the Last in 1273 in direct response to the castle erected by the English at Montgomery, but also to keep an eye on the Princes of Powys. Dolforwyn was destroyed by Edward I just four years later and by 1398 the castle, which had been roughly built, was a total ruin.

According to legend it was below the castle that soldiers pushed Princess Sabrina into the river on the order of her enraged stepmother. She did not drown, but became Goddess of the river, which is named after her. In Welsh, the name Sabrina is Hafren and in English, Severn.

After **Abermule**, the canal runs parallel with the A483. At **Brynderwen** (Bridge 146), cross the canal to pass Brynderwen Wharf, a former coal wharf, as the towpath changes banks. A short way further on, the Way crosses another bridge, and doubles back to pass beneath it to resume the towpath walk.

Beyond Brynderwen, it is towpath all the way to Welshpool, a long stretch of agreeable, easy walking, never far from the A483, but delightful nonetheless. A number of bridges add interest: Glanhafren Bridge is the most ornate, with its cast iron balustrades, while Red House Bridge is one of the few remaining swing bridges on the canal.

South of **Fron**, the canal finally meets the A-road. Cross with care to a gate opposite, and continue on the other side. Bridge 140 has an interesting benchmark affixed to it, number 12047, one of a series introduced by Ordnance Survey in the 1920s.

North of Fron, the canal (but not the towpath) passes beneath the A-road. Walk out to cross the road and continue beside the on-going canal. Press on to the edge of **Garthmyl**, to meet the **B4385**. Turn left to a T-junction with the A-road, and go right, passing the Nags Head, then bear left into a side road to a bridge. Once across the bridge, drop immediately left to relocate the canal.

The Severn Way

map continues on page 54

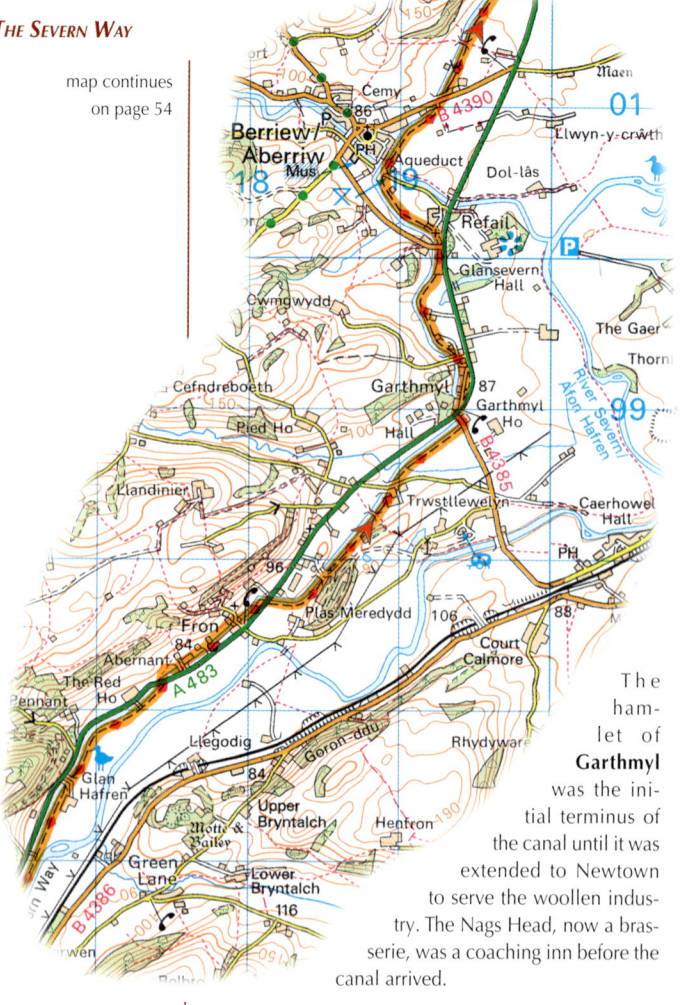

The hamlet of **Garthmyl** was the initial terminus of the canal until it was extended to Newtown to serve the woollen industry. The Nags Head, now a brasserie, was a coaching inn before the canal arrived.

Continue under Bridge 130, and bear left alongside the canal and eventually cross the **Berriew Aqueduct**, which was first built of stone, but collapsed in 1796 and had to be rebuilt in 1889. The area around the canal and aqueduct is a Site of Special Scientific

STAGE 5 – NEWTOWN TO WELSHPOOL

Canalside walking on the way to Welshpool

Interest (SSSI), because of its water plants, notably yellow iris, bur-reed, pink flowering rush, floating water plantain and sedges.

Anyone wanting to visit **Berriew** should leave the towpath at the aqueduct and descend to join a lane. Turn left alongside the River Rhiw and walk up towards the village. Go to a junction near the Talbot Hotel. Turn right, crossing the Rhiw, and a short way on are the village shops and the Lion Hotel. To resume the Way, leave the village along the B4390, to reach the canal. Berriew has a couple of pubs (the Lion Hotel and the Talbot Hotel), as well as the Lychgate Cottage tearooms.

Just north of Berriew, continue along the canal as the Breidden Hills ease briefly into view. The canal continues to pass behind the nearby Horseshoe pub, and eventually reaches the **Belan Locks**.

> Much of the land here belonged to the **Earl of Powys**, who was a major shareholder in the Montgomery Canal. The landowners in the Severn

THE SEVERN WAY

valley were prosperous and provided good housing for their workers. Waggoners lived in fine estate cottages down the lane at Sarn-y-bryn-caled. The Powys family were quick to spot the benefits that came with the Industrial Revolution, and built a model farm, called Coed-y-dinas. Water from the canal supplied steam engines that drove threshing and other machines.

At Bridge 120, the Way passes back beneath the **A458**. In 1995, the road bridge over the canal here was replaced to allow boat traffic under the new bridge. The canal was realigned, leaving a section that is the heart of Whitehouse Nature Reserve. Continue to follow the canal through the centre of **Welshpool**, to meet and cross the B4381.

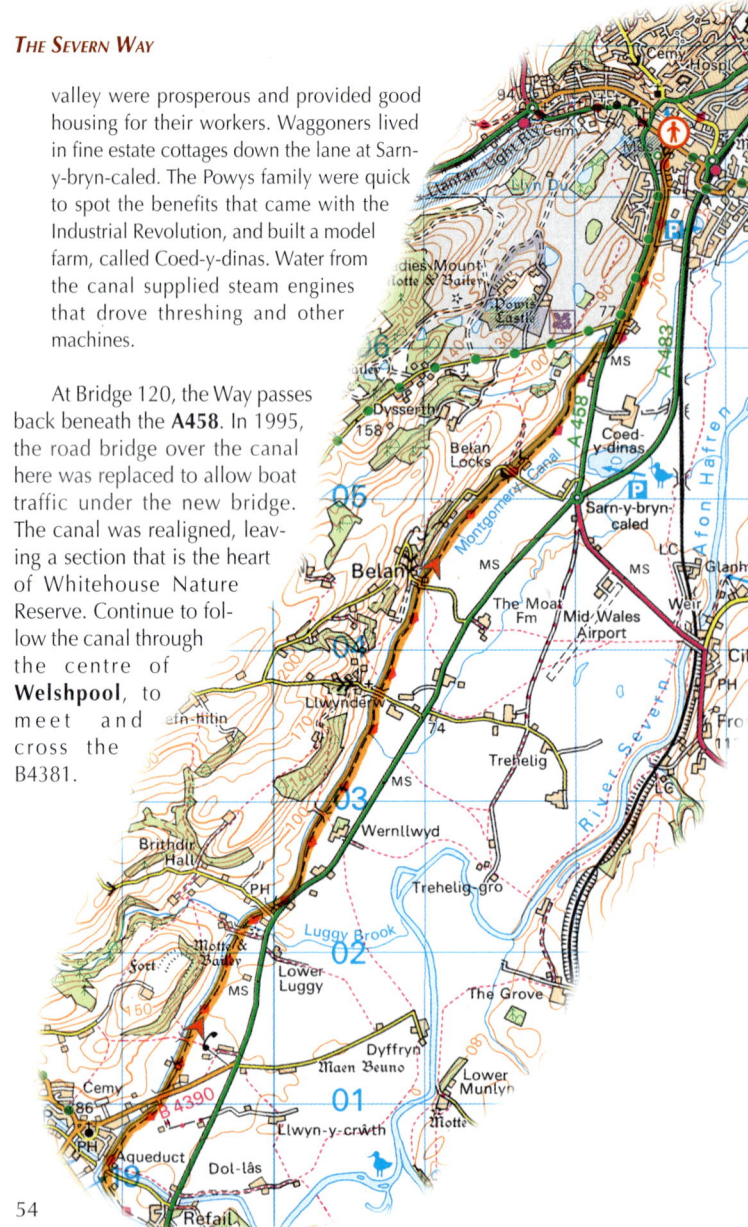

Stage 5 – Newtown to Welshpool

WELSHPOOL

The town of Welshpool (Welsh: *Y Trallwng*) became a borough in 1263 under the title of Burgus de Pola by grant of market charter from the then Prince of Powys, Gwenwynwyn. In English it was initially known as Pool, but its name was changed to Welshpool in 1835 to distinguish it from the English town of Poole. Today, the streets are lined with buildings from many periods, although it is those from the Georgian period that dominate.

Welshpool railway station is on the Cambrian Line, served by Arriva Trains Wales, and the town is the starting point of the Welshpool and Llanfair Light Railway, a narrow-gauge heritage railway popular with tourists, with its terminus station at Raven Square. The local economy is mainly based upon agriculture and local industry. The Smithfield Livestock Market (on Mondays) is the largest one-day sheep market in Europe. Severn Wayfarers will find Welshpool a convenient and welcoming overnight halt.

The Severn at Welshpool

STAGE 6
Welshpool to Crew Green

Start	Welshpool
Finish	Crew Green
Distance	18.3km (11½ miles)
Ascent	45m (140ft)
Descent	60m (200ft)

The stretch of the Severn Way from Welshpool to Crew Green, where it passes from the custody of Wales into the care of England, has two distinct sections. The first follows the towpath of the Montgomery Canal as far as Pool Quay; thereafter the route rediscovers the Severn and flirts with it at varying distances, getting to know its meandering way as it passes round the heights of the Breidden Hills. Both sections provide delightful riverside walking, the former shaded for the most part, the latter more open to the elements. Once Welshpool is left behind there is little in the way of civilisation; it is mostly farmland, pastured by cattle and longwool sheep.

The Severn Way resumes at Bridge 119, and runs on the short distance to the Lledan Aqueduct. The original masonry aqueduct of the 1790s was replaced in 1836 by the present structure, an iron trough resting on cast iron beams. The cast iron overbridge once carried the Welshpool and Llanfair Railway to sidings by the Cambrian railway station.

The canalside path leads out to the A483, before continuing on the other side soon to reach Buttington Wharf.

This was an important centre for **lime burning** and underpinned the canal's limited commercial success. Three of the lime kilns once active here are visible in the car park just a few strides from the canal towpath. The production of lime, which began here when the canal opened, was a continuous process throughout the summer. Men would load the kilns with limestone, and the lime produced was

Mute swans on the Montgomery Canal

supplied to farmers up to five miles away, to be used as fertiliser.

Eventually, the towpath and canal come out to join the A-road again, and the Severn Way is here joined by Offa's Dyke Path, which shares its route to Llandrinio. Where the

map continues on page 59

The Severn Way

two routes coincide there are no Severn Way waymarks, so those for Offa's Dyke Path should be followed.

OFFA'S DYKE

Offa's Dyke Path runs for 283km (177 miles) from Sedbury Cliffs on the Severn Estuary near Chepstow to Prestatyn in North Wales on Liverpool Bay. For about 112km (70 miles) it follows the course of the earthwork of Offa's Dyke, built on the orders of Offa, ruler of the dominant English kingdom of Mercia from 757 to 796. The dyke is the longest archaeological monument in Britain and consists mainly of a bank, with a ditch on the Welsh side. No one is certain of its purpose; it may have been defensive or may merely have been intended to define the border. It is discontinuous, and it seems that in places natural features were considered sufficient – this might explain why there is no dyke along this stretch of the Severn.

For some time the route has been moving ever closer to the Breidden Hills, and their bulky form will dominate much of this and the next day's walking.

At Top Lock at **Pool Quay** (Powys Arms – pub and B&B – accessible from the towpath) the route finally bids farewell to the Montgomery Canal, being deflected down to the right along a track to a lane, and then turns right to go down to the road.

> **Pool Quay** was a Severnside settlement originally, marking the head of navigation on the river, but only in the winter was there sufficient depth of water this far upstream. The canal provided a more reliable trade route and carrying on the river had ceased by the middle of the 19th century. Pool Quay Lock on the canal is particularly attractive, and is overlooked by a pretty Victorian church with a timber belfry.

At the road, turn left, walking for about 200m, to rejoin Offa's Dyke Path on the opposite side of the road, immediately going left over a stile, and across two fields finally rejoining the River Severn. The appearance of floodbanks may suggest that this is actually Offa's Dyke,

STAGE 6 – WELSHPOOL TO CREW GREEN

but it isn't. Once hooked up to the Severn again, the Way is never far distant as it crosses numerous fields.

Walk along the floodbank, an agreeable and easy stretch, as the route flirts with the Severn below the gaze of the shapely Breidden Hills.

map continues on page 60

> These **massive humps** dominate the landscape for miles around. The most northerly is quarry-scarred Breidden Hill itself, topped by Rodney's Pillar, an 18th-century monument to Admiral Rodney (1719–1792), who used Montgomeryshire timber for Royal Navy ships, although nationally he was more famous for defeating the French off Cape St Vincent in 1782. To the south is Moel y Golfa, which also has a memorial on top, to Ernest Burton, a Romany 'king' who died in 1960. There is another main summit, Middletown Hill, and a few smaller ones. Not surprisingly, there are Iron Age forts on the three main hills and a couple of lesser forts too.

For a while the route is deflected away from the river. Around **Rhyd-esgyn** the field pastures

THE SEVERN WAY

Llandrinio Bridge

close in and the Way follows closely by the river, past Upper House, and continues to a flood barrier, used to gain some control over the Severn in times of flood, and then heads left along an embankment to Derwas Bridge, which spans a man-made channel, the **New Cut**. Cross the bridge and turn right, crossing a field to a footbridge spanning Bele Brook, a minor tributary of the Severn.

STAGE 6 – WELSHPOOL TO CREW GREEN

Over the footbridge turn right once more, now parting company with Offa's Dyke Path, which shortly joins the actual dyke itself, heading roughly northwards to Llanymynech Hill, whose much-quarried slopes are visible ahead.

It was these quarries that provided the **limestone** which was transported on the Montgomery Canal, although Llanymynech is now better known for its abundant wild flowers. Like the Breiddens and Long Mountain, Llanymynech Hill is shared between England and Wales.

Walk along the top of a grassy embankment, and then on by an obvious path towards the village of **Llandrinio**. Walk out to meet the road at Llandrinio and turn right over the bridge to walk along the road.

LLANDRINIO

Just a little to the west is Llandrinio's Norman church, dedicated to St Trunio. In the porch there stands a fragment of a 10th-century stone cross.

Llandrinio bridge is especially attractive, and a site of much interest. This was a crossing point since Roman times (remains of a Roman road have been found to the west of the bridge), and a controlled route for trade and two millennia later a defence against invasion during World War 2, when it would have been manned by the Home Guard. In the Middle Ages, folk crossed the Severn here by ferry, and the nearby cottage was probably that of the ferry man. The bridge was built in 1775, and the road over the bridge may have been a turnpike. The south-west corner of the bridge is a disguised pillbox; the concrete blocks having been shaped to look like a farm building. But there is an opening, facing east, through which a machine gun could have controlled the approach to the bridge.

THE SEVERN WAY

Approaching Crew Green, and leaving Wales

After 450m turn left over a stile and go along a grassy embankment to pass **Lower House Farm**. The path briefly touches on the Severn again, but then shortcuts a loop before rejoining the river at the end of a long, straight embankment.

Walk on along the embankment until you meet an obvious broad track heading south to the road. Go down this as far as a sluice gate, and there turn left, once more on a raised embankment. From a stile head across a field and then descend to briefly rejoin the river, which now performs a number of serpentine loops. In the next field move away from the river, heading straight across the field, as the path shortcuts a loop. Rejoin the river and once more head across fields, passing the confluence with the **Afon Efyrnwy** (River Vyrnwy).

Go forward to pass below an iron bridge and immediately turn right to a road. Turn right again, over the bridge. As you cross the Severn at **Crew Green**, you are leaving Wales and entering the English county of Shropshire.

SHROPSHIRE

The Severn banks at Ditherington

The Severn Way

Shrewsbury Castle

By the time the Severn enters Shropshire it has matured into a lazily meandering river cut deeply into its floodplain. One of its meanders virtually encircles the town of Shrewsbury, and, one day, if Nature has its way, will turn it into an island. From the moment of entering Shropshire at Crew Green to leaving it at Upper Arley, the walking is of the easiest kind, with only minor undulations.

Crew Green is significant for walkers on the Severn Way, for it is here that the route passes from Wales into England. Initially, a mix of farmland paths and minor lanes follows, with precious little in the way of views of the River Severn, but eventually the Severn is rejoined and followed throughout this section. For the most part it is gentle walking, with extended stretches along quiet country lanes close by the river, and bright in springtime with wild flowers and birds. There is a pub in Crew Green (the Fir Tree Inn), and Brookhouse Farm provides a B&B halt for the night.

STAGE 7
Crew Green to Montford Bridge

Start	Crew Green
Finish	Montford Bridge
Distance	13.9km (8¾ miles)
Ascent	70m (230ft)
Descent	70m (230ft)

St Peter's Church, Melverley

Cross the iron bridge and immediately branch left over a stile. Then, straight away bear right to a metal gate and fence and head for **Melverley**, walking along the top of a raised section between arable fields. Off to the left, the Breidden Hills loom darkly, pinned in place by Rodney's Pillar.

When the raised section finally ends at a step-stile beyond another gate, cross a rough pasture to a group of farm buildings. Swing right here and join a road by the delightful St Peter's Church, to which a visit is recommended.

MELVERLEY AND ST PETER'S CHURCH

Melverley was situated on the Shropshire & Montgomeryshire Light Railway Line, a route designed to link Shrewsbury with the small village of Llanymynech, near Oswestry. A viaduct took the line across the Severn, but this fell into the river in 1902. It was rebuilt to enable the re-opening of the line in April 1911, but was subsequently deemed unsafe on a number of occasions and was a contributory factor in the demise of the line.

On the ecclesiastical front, by late Saxon times there was already a chapel at Melverley, but in 1401 this was destroyed by Owain Glyndwr. Almost immediately, work started on a replacement, and by 1406 a new church was standing on the site. Dedicated to St Peter, it still survives and remains substantially unaltered except for interior embellishment and repairs. It's a very rare example of a timber, wattle and daub church, one of only three such churches to be found in Shropshire and the oldest of its kind. All the original beams,

THE SEVERN WAY

> made from local oak, are fixed together with wooden pegs, and no nails were used at all. There is a small Saxon font, which must have stood in the original church, while the altar and finely carved pulpit are Jacobean.

From the church, walk out to a T-junction close by the Tontine Inn.

The **Tontine Inn** (01691 682258), like many others throughout Britain, is named after an interesting legal arrangement. A tontine is an investment plan for raising capital, one that was devised in the 17th century and became widespread during the 18th and 19th centuries. Under a tontine arrangement, each subscriber pays an agreed sum into the fund, and receives an annuity. As members die, their shares devolve to the other participants, and so the value of each annuity increases. On the death of the last member, the scheme is wound up. There is a variant on this arrangement under which, on the death of the penultimate member, the capital passes to the last survivor. This recipe for the 'accidental demise' of shareholders has provided the plot for many fictional tales. Another Tontine Inn will be passed in Stourport.

Cross the road and a stile opposite, and head across a

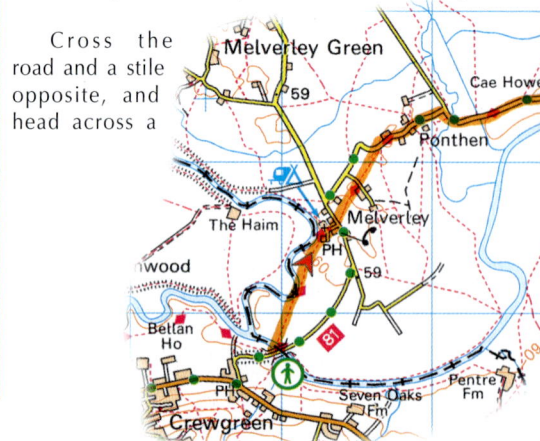

Stage 7 – Crew Green to Montford Bridge

number of fields until you meet a lane. Turn right, walking towards Pentre. The Way goes through **Ponthen** before branching right for Pentre. Go past **Cae Howel Farm** and at the next road junction go left, walking towards Edgerley for about 100m to a step-stile on the right, into a paddock. Cross the edge of this and a rough pasture beyond to enter a caravan site. (The Royal Hill Inn, overlooking the Severn, is a short distance along the Pentre road from the Edgerley turning.)

On entering the caravan park go forward, continuing in roughly the same direction on a broad track through trees to a step-stile into a large field. Strike across the middle of the field towards the far right-hand corner, and through a hedge gap and out to a lane. Go diagonally right across the lane to a concealed stile. Cross beside a fence to another stile, and then bear half-right across rough pasture to another concealed stile. Over this, bear half-right towards a gated hedge gap, to locate two stiles close together. After the second, cross one last field targeting a distant red brick

map continues on page 68

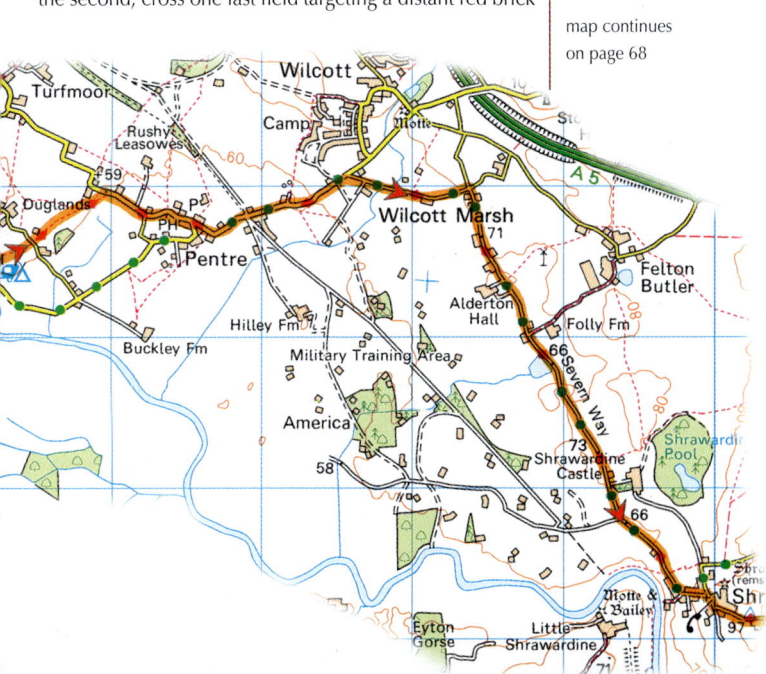

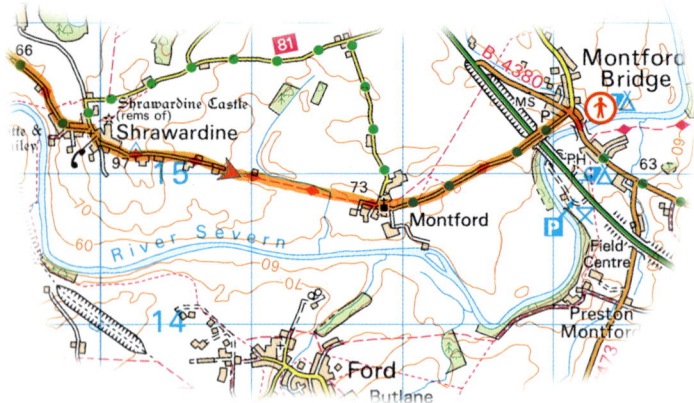

house, near which a stile gives onto a lane. Turn right, through **Pentre** and on along the road.

Just after the entrance to Nesscliff Training Camp at **Wilcott Marsh**, turn right for Shrawardine, following the lane past **Alderton Hall** and Folly Pool to the village.

The area on the right is farmland, but is used for **military training**. During World War 2 the Central Ammunition Storage Depot was sited here.

SHRAWARDINE

Shrawardine is an attractive place of timber-framed cottages and a sandstone church, St Mary's, which is partly Norman, although much restored and rebuilt. Shrawardine Castle now consists only of a mound, part of a ditch and fragments of masonry in a field on the east side of the village. The earliest castle on this site was probably built soon after the Norman Conquest by Rainald the Sheriff, whom the Domesday survey records as holding the manor of Shrawardine. It later became a Royal castle, serving as an outpost of Shrewsbury, and was destroyed by the Welsh in 1215. It was rebuilt after 1220 and what survives today is from that period. The castle was dismantled by Oliver Cromwell's troops in 1645, after a siege lasting just five days.

Having passed Shrawardine church, at a junction turn right (signposted 'No Through Road'), and shortly follow the road round as it bends to the left. Keep on to the end of the road surfacing, and then go forward onto a green lane that leads across farmland into **Montford** and comes out just by St Chad's Church.

MONTFORD

This small, quiet village was formerly part of the huge Powis Estate, centred on Powis Castle in Welshpool. The square-towered sandstone St Chad's church occupies a dominant position on high ground above the river, with fine views to the Breidden Hills. It's a relatively recent building, dating from the mid-18th century, and designed by a Shrewsbury man, William Cooper.

The parents of naturalist Charles Darwin – Robert Waring Darwin and Susannah Darwin – are buried in the churchyard, as is his sister, Susan. Robert was the son of Erasmus Darwin, a prominent physician, poet and freethinker who anticipated his grandson's views on evolution. Susannah was the daughter of Josiah Wedgwood, the potter.

Pass the church and continue along the lane, which leads over the **A5** to a crossroads at the riverside settlement of **Montford Bridge**.

STAGE 8
Montford Bridge to Shrewsbury (English Bridge)

Start	Montford Bridge
Finish	Shrewsbury (English Bridge)
Distance	10.8km (6¾ miles)
Ascent	100m (320ft)
Descent	105m (340ft)

Between Montford Bridge and Shelton on the outskirts of Shrewsbury, the Severn loops northwards in serpentine fashion that would add 15.5km (9½ miles) to the walk if it could be followed. Instead, the route takes a shortcut, the only possible route, across pleasant farmland, by quiet hedgeways and tracks, and below skies patrolled by buzzards.

Turn right on reaching the **B4380** at Montford Bridge, soon passing an angular toll house (on the left), and then crossing the Severn. Just opposite the Wingfield Arms, turn left onto a brief track leading to a field gate. Now go forward to pass along the rear of houses. On the far side of the field a bridge crosses a stream and gives onto a footpath around a field edge. Follow this as far as a gate on the left onto a cycle track. Walk directly upfield, keeping to the right of a mid-field oak tree. At the top edge of the field, take the right-hand one of two metal field gates, giving onto a green track between hedgerows that leads to a surfaced lane.

Keep forward, and soon pass an old yew-enshrouded churchyard next to Bicton Hall that encloses the ruins of a 16th-century church. A cluster of cottages and farms completes the hamlet, often known as **Old Bicton** to distinguish it from the modern village which has grown up nearby around a church built in 1885.

Follow the lane until it bends to the right in front of Woodland Cottages. Leave it just after the bend, through a gate on the left, and follow a bridleway to Grove Farm, beyond which a lane leads to a T-junction at Rossall Lodge. Cross the road and join a path to the right of the

STAGE 8 – MONTFORD BRIDGE TO SHREWSBURY (ENGLISH BRIDGE)

Lodge, going through gates and across a small paddock before striking across a field by a waymarked route. On the other side, beyond two bridlegates, field edge paths now lead on across fields. Eventually a brace of gates gives onto a wooded path leading out to a broad track. Keep following the track, until it runs out to meet the B4380 at **Shelton**.

Turn left at the road and 100m further on go left again, down a bridleway that descends as a broad track into broadleaved woodland, before continuing as a holloway, eventually to meet an estate road at Mountwood Park. Keep forward, ascending, and soon branch left onto a parallel, enclosed path, which shortly runs high above the Severn, to which it gradually descends. The river is now followed all the way to **Shrewsbury**, a relaxing and genial stretch.

The Severn at Shrewsbury

SHREWSBURY

The market hall

It was the River Severn that determined Shrewsbury's siting, its development and, to a large extent, its character. Known to the ancient Britons as Pengwern, and to Anglo-Saxons as Scrobbesburth (or Scrobbesbyrig), the town was built within the natural moat provided by a tight loop of the Severn, completely encircled except for a small gap, making a perfect defensive site. Even the gap was guarded by a ridge, on which a castle was later built. Soon after the Norman Conquest, King William gave much of Shropshire to Roger de Montgomery, creating him Earl of Shrewsbury. Roger built a substantial castle and for many years the town was a base for Norman operations against the Welsh. At the same time, however, it was building on its riverside location to become a busy inland port. By the 14th century, despite involvement in border conflicts, it was one of the wealthiest towns in England, successful in a variety of trades. It was the woollen cloth trade, however, which assumed pre-eminence and it remained Shrewsbury's staple until the end of the 18th century, reaching its peak in the Tudor period after peace with Wales had finally been achieved. It was the wool merchants and

Stage 8 – Montford Bridge to Shrewsbury (English Bridge)

drapers who built many of the spectacular timber-framed mansions which still grace Shrewsbury's streets today.

Following the disruption of the Civil Wars (1642–1651), and a gradual decline in the wool trade, Shrewsbury became a fashionable centre for leisure and shopping, a role which expanded in the great coaching era, thanks to the town's position on the main London–Holyhead road. As elsewhere throughout Britain, the coming of the railways killed both road and river traffic but opened up new opportunities. With the subsequent decline of the railways, Shrewsbury has fallen prey to the usual traffic congestion, but remains an important regional centre.

For today's visitor, much of Shrewsbury's charm derives from the survival of its largely unaltered medieval street pattern, particularly the abundance of narrow passages known locally as shuts and gullets. There's a great deal to see, with a total of 660 listed buildings in the town centre alone. Few places have such an astonishing wealth of period buildings and the impact is all the greater because most are crowded together in the centre, within the Severn's tight embrace.

Here is no place for an exhaustive list of Shrewsbury's attractions, but a few highlights might include its medieval churches, the best of which is St Mary's, a mixture of many periods, but originally of Saxon foundation. The ancient centre of Shrewsbury is St Alkmund's Square, where there are two churches of Saxon origin, both rebuilt in the 18th century.

One of Shrewsbury's most famous sons is, of course, Charles Darwin, who attended Shrewsbury School, a superb building founded by Edward VI in 1552. Darwin's statue sits outside it, but it is now Shrewsbury Library, the school having moved across the river to Kingsland in 1882. Almost opposite the library is one of the finest of all provincial railway stations, a masterpiece of Victorian 'Tudor'. Nearby is the castle – not Roger de Montgomery's original but a later one, remodelled by Thomas Telford.

Other notable buildings include Bear Steps, the Council House Gatehouse, Abbot's House, Ireland's Mansion, Owen's Mansion and Rowley's House. Some of the finest streets are Butcher Row, Dogpole, Wyle Cop, Claremont Hill, High Street, Fish Street and Milk Street. But this only briefly touches on the splendour of Shrewsbury; wherever you look there is a wealth of interest.

Economically, Shrewsbury serves as a cultural and commercial centre for the county of Shropshire and for a large area of mid-Wales, being only 14km (9 miles) east of the Welsh border.

THE SEVERN WAY

En route, the Way enters **Doctor's Field Countryside Heritage Site**. Directly above the field stands The Mount, birthplace in 1809 of Charles Darwin. The land was owned by his father, a prominent local person, but the name 'Doctor's Field' is older than the Darwin family, and is of uncertain origin.

Beyond Doctor's Field, the path runs between fences, and ends by climbing steps. At the top, turn left onto a walled path bordered by houses. Another flight of steps descends to follow a path at the rear of gardens, later rising to the edge of Shrewsbury County Cricket Ground, formerly known as 'Gooseland', although the Old English word *Gos* also refers to swans.

Continue around the playing field, heading for Frankwell footbridge and Theatre Severn and then continue by the river to pass under the graceful Welsh Bridge, built in its present form in 1795, although there was a bridge here soon after 1100. The riverside path, graced by mature weeping willows, eventually leads up Water Lane to a road. Turn left, go past the Boat House Inn, and then left over Port Hill Bridge, a handsome suspension bridge of 1922. On the other side turn right and follow the river, passing under Kingsland Bridge and Greyfriars Bridge before reaching English Bridge, built in 1774, and rebuilt in 1925, although the Severn was first spanned here in about 1100.

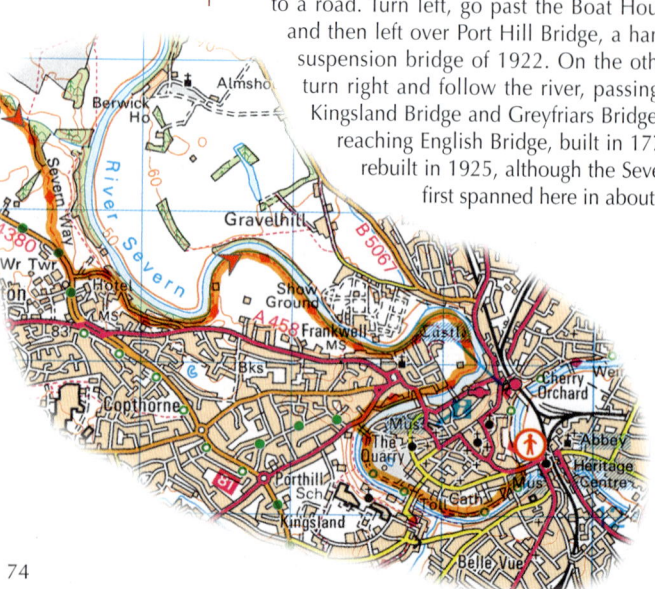

STAGE 9
Shrewsbury (English Bridge) to Atcham

Start	Shrewsbury (English Bridge)
Finish	Atcham
Distance	12.3km (7¾ miles)
Ascent	60m (200ft)
Descent	70m (220ft)

Even a cursory study of maps shows how valid it was for AE Housman to describe Shrewsbury (in *A Shropshire Lad*) as 'islanded in Severn stream'; the time will come, no doubt, when the Severn cuts through the 270m of land separating Mountfields and the railway station, making its own shortcut and leaving Shrewsbury surrounded by an ox-bow lake, truly 'islanded'.

Once the urban influence of Shrewsbury is left behind, then not even the various A-road and railway crossings detract from what is essentially a lovely, if serpentine, walk. The river is, for most of the year, a sedate companion not leaving the Way until Atcham is reached.

Continue along the riverside walkway from English Bridge, and on to pass beneath the railway, continuing to a road just beyond a weir. Keep forward, and when the road bends left pass through a gate onto a narrow stony path through trees beside the river.

At the bridge linking **Ditherington** to Monkmoor, climb steps and cross the bridge, descending on the other side and turning beneath the

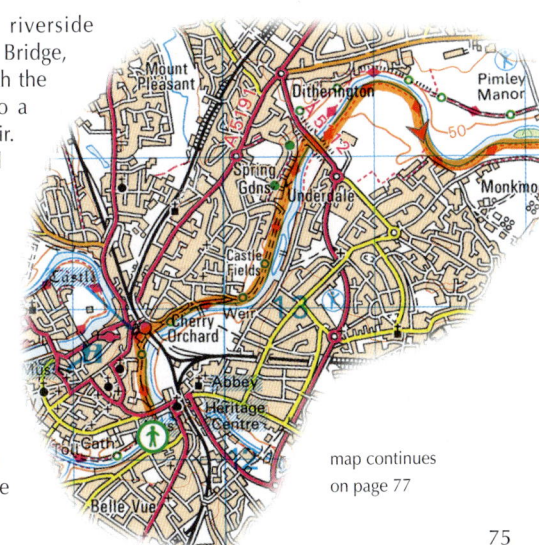

map continues on page 77

English Bridge, Shrewsbury

bridge to join a path along the true right bank of the river as it now meanders onwards past **Monkmoor**, and eventually passing below the **A49**.

MONKMOOR AND UFFINGTON

The village of Uffington comes into view on the far bank. Uffington and Monkmoor were formerly linked by ferry at this point, but this no longer operates.

Monkmoor is where the war poet Wilfred Owen (1893–1918), born in Oswestry, lived as a boy in the early years of the 20th century. He and his family enjoyed Sunday walks by the Severn and would often take the ferry to Uffington to attend services at the village church. Owen's shocking and realistic war poetry on the horrors of the trenches and gas warfare was heavily influenced by his friend Siegfried Sassoon, and stood in stark contrast to both the public perception of war at the time and to the confidently patriotic output already published by other war poets.

Beyond Uffington rises flat-topped Haughmond Hill, covered in Forestry Commission plantations and a popular place for walks and picnics.

STAGE 9 – SHREWSBURY (ENGLISH BRIDGE) TO ATCHAM

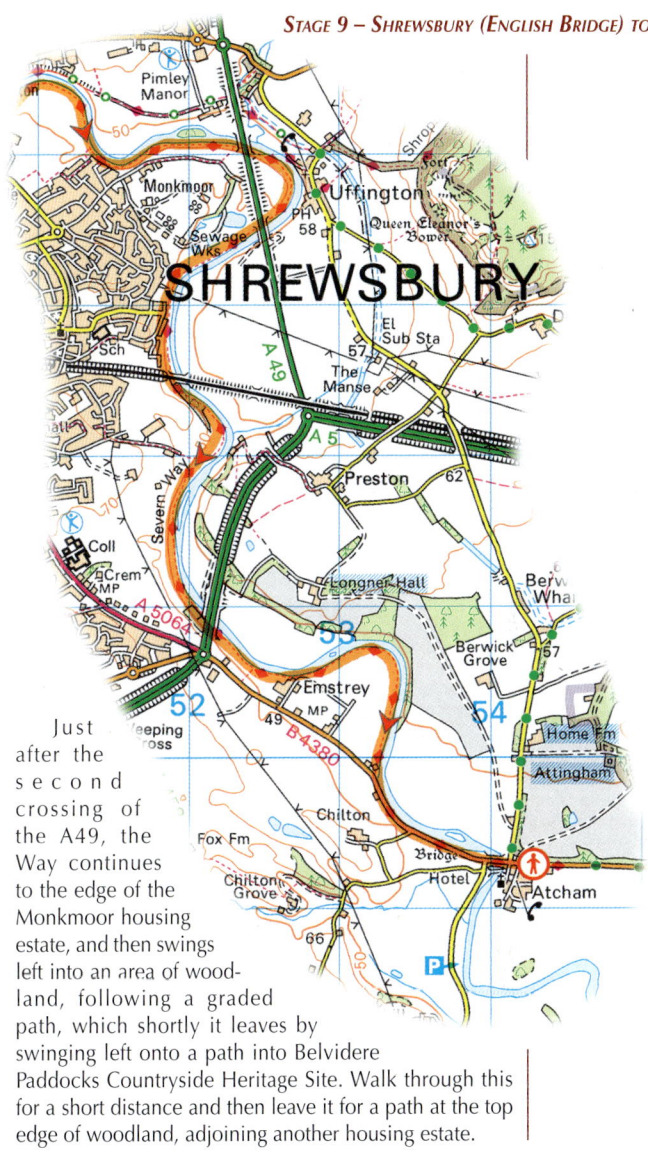

Just after the second crossing of the A49, the Way continues to the edge of the Monkmoor housing estate, and then swings left into an area of woodland, following a graded path, which shortly it leaves by swinging left onto a path into Belvidere Paddocks Countryside Heritage Site. Walk through this for a short distance and then leave it for a path at the top edge of woodland, adjoining another housing estate.

ATCHAM

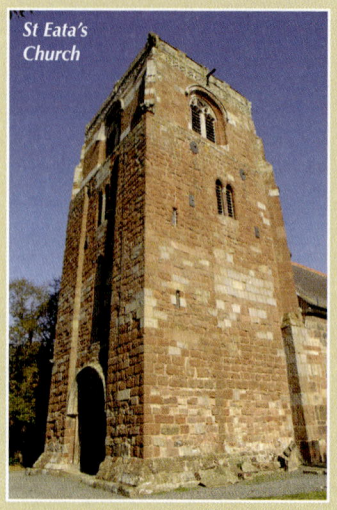

St Eata's Church

Atcham is a small village distinguished notably by the presence of Attingham Park, a National Trust property built to the design of George Steuart in 1785 for Noel Hill, first Lord Berwick. One of Shropshire's grandest houses, it has a magnificent Regency interior and is surrounded by parkland landscaped by the renowned Humphrey Repton.

On a much more human scale, however, is St Eata's Church, which stands by the Severn. It was built in the 11th century, although what remains is mostly of later construction, and is the only church in Britain dedicated to the Celtic St Eata, one of St Aidan's disciples at Lindisfarne, who was consecrated Bishop of North Northumbria in AD678, and became Bishop of Hexham in AD685. It has always been recognised that the foundation of the church was Saxon, and much of the north wall is clearly of Saxon construction, built with stones brought from the Roman town of Viroconium. The arched west door is of simple design and very attractive.

Close to the church is a handsome Georgian hotel, the Mytton and Mermaid (Jack Mytton was one of Shropshire's more notorious characters), and there are interesting cottages in the village. There are also two bridges spanning the Severn. The good-looking but redundant one was built in the 1770s by John Gwynne, the Shrewsbury architect who also designed English Bridge, the famous Magdalen Bridge at Oxford, and Worcester Bridge, which is crossed in a few days' time as the Way heads south. The other bridge was built in the 1920s.

The path descends to rejoin the riverbank. Go under the impressive Belvidere Bridge, which carries the Shrewsbury–Birmingham railway. At nearby Preston Boats, a rope ferry used to operate above an old fish weir originally owned by Haughmond Abbey. Either side of the railway bridge, the path passes through scrubby woodland shade, most welcome on a warm day; perhaps less so in rain. When it forks, branch left, staying by the river. On emerging from the woodland, press on and eventually pass beneath the **A5**. Shortly afterwards The Wrekin, a hill and well-known landmark, slips into view directly ahead.

Continue past **Emstrey Farm** and soon rejoin a riverside path, looping around the edge of farmland, before finally emerging on the **B4380** Wroxeter road. Turn left to **Atcham**.

STAGE 10

Atcham to Ironbridge

Start	Atcham
Finish	Ironbridge
Distance	19km (12 miles)
Ascent	225m (750ft)
Descent	200m (660ft)

Between Atcham and Cressage the Severn Way almost entirely follows roads. Most are quiet, pleasant and relatively traffic-free, but care needs to be taken against approaching vehicles throughout this stretch. Although the route bypasses it, a short detour to the Roman town of Viroconium is worthwhile, which now boasts a reconstructed Roman town house.

Beyond Sheinton peaceful woodland and farmland pastures lead towards the superb abbey ruins at Buildwas. After that, the former industrial town of Ironbridge awaits, reached by mainly riverside paths dominated by the cooling towers of the Buildwas Power Station.

From Atcham, continue along the B4380, which branches right soon after crossing the **River Tern**. About 500m later turn right again onto a narrow lane that leads to a T-junction on the edge of **Wroxeter** (Wroxeter Hotel nearby). A right turn takes you through the village and on along the Severn Way. Alternatively, turn left, and then left again, to visit the remains of the Roman city at Viroconium.

VIROCONIUM

Roman remains at Wroxeter

The remains of Viroconium are in the care of English Heritage and open to the public. The excavated site is relatively small, but at its zenith Viroconium was the fourth largest Roman town in Britain. It began as a military camp during the first century, but when the legion was moved to Chester about 30 years later the site was developed as a civil town. Most of the visible remains are of the second-century municipal baths, but the size of these gives an indication of the scale of the town. Also uncovered are parts of the exercise hall, market hall and forum. Still standing is an impressive section of a basilica wall, known as the 'Old Work'. Aerial photography has demonstrated, by means of crop marks, the presence of streets, houses and fortifications beneath the surface of the surrounding farmland. After the Romans left it seems that urban life continued at Viroconium until perhaps the seventh century, but it was eventually abandoned and regarded only as a useful source of building stone.

Back in Wroxeter, St Andrew's Church is also of interest. Part of the nave is Saxon and built with stone from Viroconium. The font is believed to be made from part of a Roman column and the churchyard gateposts are Roman too. There are some attractive houses in the village, and earthworks in the neighbouring fields are part of Viroconium's defences.

STAGE 10 – ATCHAM TO IRONBRIDGE

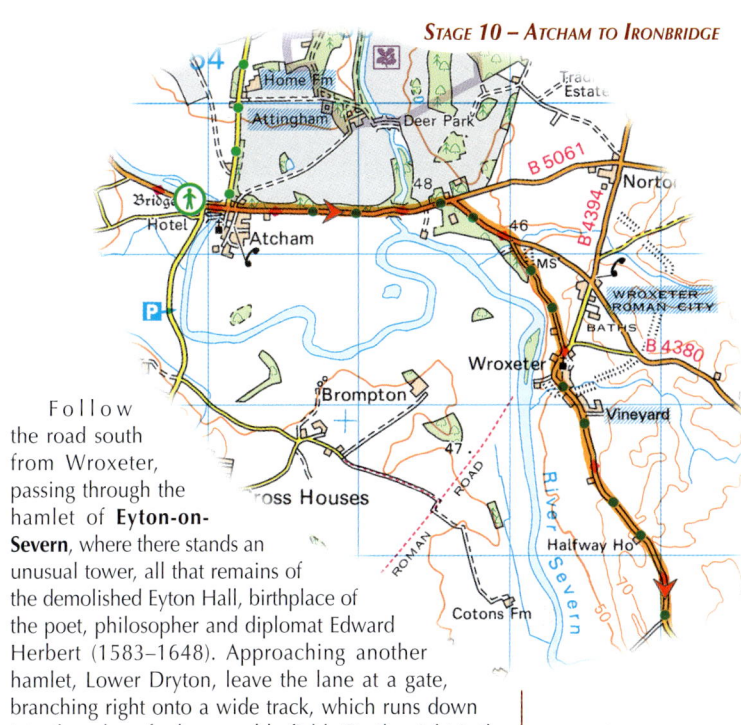

Follow the road south from Wroxeter, passing through the hamlet of **Eyton-on-Severn**, where there stands an unusual tower, all that remains of the demolished Eyton Hall, birthplace of the poet, philosopher and diplomat Edward Herbert (1583–1648). Approaching another hamlet, Lower Dryton, leave the lane at a gate, branching right onto a wide track, which runs down into the edge of a large arable field. On the right is the unexpected sight of a **National Hunt Racecourse**.

Turn left and cross two fields. About 200m into the second field, go left through a hedgerow. In the ensuing pasture, turn right alongside a fence, and then bear left on a narrow path, climbing to a waymark post on a small rise. From the waymark, cross to the corner of the field, at the left-hand edge of woodland.

Follow a track to the far side of the woodland then turn right and walk diagonally across an arable field, aiming for the left edge of a woodland boundary ahead. Reaching a stile, cross it and turn left through scrub. On the far side the Way emerges into a long, narrow riverside field and follows the Severn to Cressage Bridge. Cross the bridge and walk up to a road junction near the war memorial in **Cressage**.

map continues on page 82

THE SEVERN WAY

The village of Cressage has a pub (The Eagles), and it is claimed that the Pope's emissary St Augustine preached to the Welsh bishops in AD584 under the **Cressage Oak** (originally Christ's Oak, from which the village name derives), which stood for centuries on the site now occupied by the war memorial.

At the war memorial, turn left onto Sheinton Road, walking for some distance to reach the village of **Sheinton**. In the Domesday Book it is called Schentune or Scentune, and was held by Ralph de Mortemer. Pass Sheinton church of St Peter and St Paul, a Grade II listed building, perched above the road. The earliest parts of the church date from the 14th century. However, most of what survives today dates from Victorian times, when much of the church was rebuilt.

Buildwas Abbey

Climb steadily eastwards out of the village. Almost 1km (about half a mile) further on, as the road levels and then bends gently to the right, leave it by branching left down a surfaced driveway to **Buildwas Park**. Just on reaching a house, leave the driveway and cross a stile, descending into the delightful broadleaved woodland of Piner's Coppice. At the end of the woodland, the path runs out into an ascending track past Park

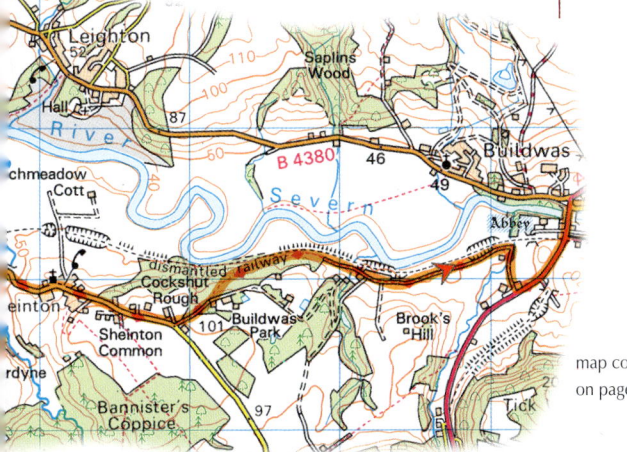

map continues on page 84

Farm and then along a surfaced track that eventually circles round Mill Farm to meet the **A4169**. Turn left, soon passing **Buildwas Abbey**.

> Another English Heritage property, **Buildwas Abbey** was a Cistercian abbey founded in 1135 as a daughter house of Furness Abbey in Cumbria. The surviving buildings date from around 1200 and the most substantial remains are of the church, famous for its superb nave arcades, and the chapter house, with its fine vaulted roof.
>
> The abbey owned many outlying farms and even had its own ironworks, a precursor of the later industrial development at Coalbrookdale and Ironbridge.

Cross Buildwas Bridge and turn right down Buildwas Road towards Ironbridge. After 250m leave the road at a gate, entering a riverside meadow. Follow the riverbank to a path that wanders through woodland sandwiched between the river and the road onto which it shortly emerges. Turn right to cross an access road, and soon drop back into rough pasture. A short way further on, the path once again comes out to run alongside the road, before returning towards the river. Eventually you pass beneath the impressive Albert Edward Bridge, built by John Fowler in 1863. Today it carries only coal trains fuelling the power station.

STAGE 10 – ATCHAM TO IRONBRIDGE

Pass Ironbridge Rowing Club to enter **Ironbridge** at Dale End Park. When you reach the Ironbridge Antiques Centre keep to the right, continuing a pleasant walk beside the river until forced out to the road. Turn right.

IRONBRIDGE

It was at Coalbrookdale in 1709 that Abraham Darby discovered that coke could be used instead of charcoal for smelting iron. It sounds a small thing, but it sparked a revolution that changed the world. Suddenly, iron could be made cheaply in large quantities, instead of being dependent on the slow, laborious process of charcoal production. It was Darby's grandson, Abraham III, who constructed the world's first iron bridge. Cast in 1779, it still spans the Severn just south of Coalbrookdale, at the place now known to the world as Ironbridge.

For a time the Ironbridge Gorge was the world's foremost industrial centre until it declined in the face of competition from the Black Country and South Wales. The industrial scars have healed and the gorge is invitingly green once more, but since the 1960s those industrial relics which do survive have been transformed into a collection of fascinating and innovative museums, and Ironbridge is now a Unesco-designated World Heritage Site.

The Iron Bridge

THE SEVERN WAY

STAGE 11
Ironbridge to Bridgnorth

Start	Ironbridge
Finish	Bridgnorth
Distance	14.8km (9¼ miles)
Ascent	205m (680ft)
Descent	235m (770ft)

Between the industrial legacy that is Ironbridge, and the market town of Bridgnorth, the Severn Way largely follows closely along the course of the river. After an initial stretch following an old railway trackbed, beyond Coalport it runs along the river bank. Fields, woodlands, silent anglers, birdlife and little else occupy the day in a tranquil and enjoyable interlude.

It's well worth exploring Ironbridge. Despite its popularity as a tourist destination, it remains unspoilt. The actual Iron Bridge is a graceful structure and the focal point of the town.

Between Apley Forge and Bridgnorth the route hugs the riverbank, and provides easy walking along a pleasant, peaceful and particularly well-wooded stretch of the Severn. Kingfishers and grey wagtails frequent the river, and cormorants are present in autumn and winter.

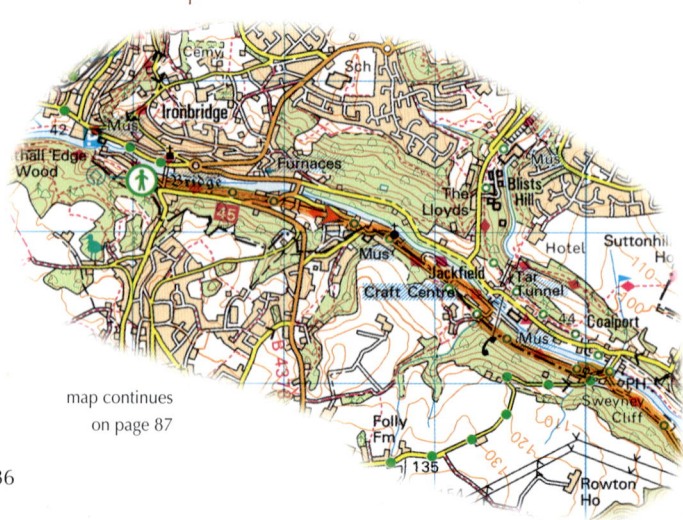

map continues on page 87

STAGE 11 – IRONBRIDGE TO BRIDGNORTH

Cross the Iron Bridge, noting the scale of toll charges at the former tollhouse above the right bank, and turn left through the car park that has replaced the railway station. On the far side, join the former railway trackbed, walking through pleasant mixed woodland that offers welcome shade on a warm day.

> The railway was the **Severn Valley line**, which was completed in 1862 and ran from Shrewsbury to Hartlebury (near Droitwich), 64km (40 miles) away.

On reaching a road at an old level crossing gate (said to be the widest in Britain), keep right on an ascending lane that rises into Church Road. Go past the entrance to the Jackfield Tile Museum, bearing left onto the lower of two lanes, and soon passing Jackfield Village Hall and the church of St Mary the Virgin.

At the roadhead, go left down a stony track into woodland and to the riverbank and then onto a path rising through scrubby woodland. Meeting a lane at a bend, go left towards a former pub, and just past it turn up a brief grassy path onto a tarmac path at the rear of properties that leads out to the **Maws Craft Centre**, housed in the surviving buildings of what was once the largest encaustic tile works in the world. Today, the centre comprises over 20 individual workshops housing a wide variety of art, craft and design businesses, in the Victorian factory of Maw & Co.

Keep forward alongside the centre and on into Ferry Road, passing terraced cottages, the Boat Inn (note the flood levels marked on its door) and the War Memorial Bridge.

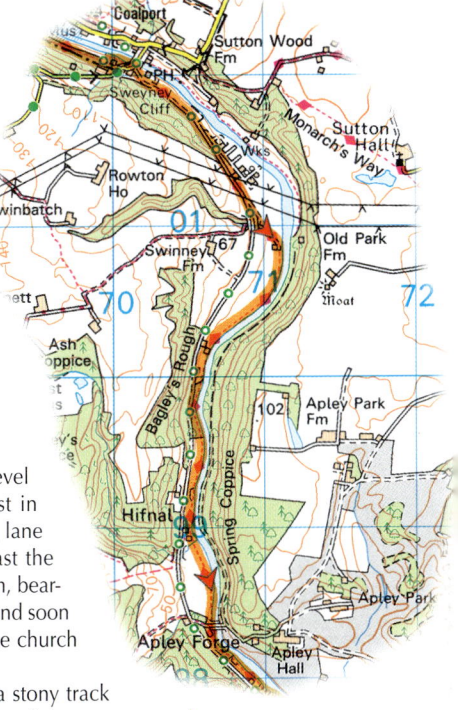

map continues on page 88

The Severn Way

COALPORT

A short detour across the footbridge visits Coalport, where facilities include pubs and a youth hostel. Coalport Bridge, now cast iron, was originally wooden. There is much of historical interest here, including Coalport China Museum, next to which a stop lock and a short stretch of water are all that remain of the Coalport section of the Shropshire Canal, built in 1788–1792 by ironmaster William Reynolds to link local mines and ironworks with the Severn. Close to the footbridge is the Hay Inclined Plane, a major industrial monument. It was the means by which boats were transferred between canals, carried up and down the 1-in-3 gradient on wheeled cradles.

Just past the Boat Inn, follow the road as it rises to the right, and pass under a railway bridge, then turn right, up steps to the trackbed, and right again to follow the trackbed for some distance. Eventually the lovely wooded route is deflected left by a couple of cottages, descending to a riverside path, which later leads to a couple of tables that comprise Preen's Eddy Picnic Area, and on to a road at Coalport Bridge, near the Woodbridge Inn.

Turn right, walking up the road to the old station, there turning left along

Field edge walking on the way to Apley Forge

a concrete-surfaced lane (the course of the dismantled railway) as far as a Severn Trent **waterworks**, just beyond which the Way branches left through a metal gate and onto a descending track. Keep left at a railway bridge and press on to the edge of an arable field and then on to meet the riverbank once more, at Foundry Cottage (the site of a former ironworks). Beyond, amble pleasantly along the riverside path, passing briefly in and out of woodland, and on to **Apley Forge** and its elegant footbridge.

APLEY FORGE

There are just a few Victorian cottages at Apley Forge today and it's hard to imagine that this sublimely peaceful place was once the scene of industry, with two forges in operation (the site of Upper Forge is just a short distance away, a little further up Linley Brook). The surrounding woods – Rookery, Boat and Chestnut coppices – were harvested to provide sustainable supplies of fuel for the forges. The practice of coppicing (cutting trees to ground level on a regular cycle of around ten years) was once commonplace, and ensured a continual crop of timber.

A handsome, white-painted suspension bridge built soon after 1900 spans the river at Apley, and was built to link Apley Park with Linley Station on the Severn Valley Railway. The bridge is private, providing no public access to the east bank. The former station house is just to the north of Apley Forge.

Across the river, set in beautiful Apley Park, below the steep, wooded cliffs of Apley Terrace, stands Apley Hall, which has seen use as a boarding school and a retirement home. A large, castellated, English Gothic Revival house of Grinshill stone, Apley Hall was built for Bridgnorth MP Thomas Whitmore in 1811, incorporating an older Georgian house, which itself stood on the site of a house built in 1308. It was also home to the Foster and Avery families. The Hall is a Grade II* listed building, claimed to be one of the largest in the county of Shropshire.

The hall is said to have been the inspiration for PG Wodehouse's famous Blanding's Castle. Wodehouse stayed briefly at the hall, and its many Gothic pinnacles, lancet windows and castellation made it the ideal inspiration for his comic duo Jeeves and Wooster. In 2004 the house was sold to specialist developers who have since divided the Hall into several self-contained apartments.

Beyond Chestnut Coppice you pass some rock houses hollowed out of a small sandstone bluff; they are seasonally obscured by foliage and are easily missed. The sandstone in this area, and downriver almost as far as Worcester, lends itself to this treatment, and there are plenty more such man-made caves, many of which were lived in until comparatively recently, even, in some cases, into the 1960s.

The continuation is always now close by the river, until, on approaching Bridgnorth, the route runs for some distance along the edge of a golf fairway (with attendant risk of flying golf balls), while the far bank rises to sheer, pine-clad, sandstone cliffs. High Rock and Pendlestone Rock are especially impressive.

Below Pendlestone Rock look out for the bizarre **Fort Pendlestone**. Rebuilt in its present form by William Whitmore of Apley Hall in the 19th century, it has had many uses, including an industrial estate.

Reaching the edge of town, you join a road and continue in front of new houses built on the site of a medieval friary.

Approaching Bridgnorth

The **friary** was established by the Franciscan Order between 1224 and 1244 and documentary evidence shows that both Henry III and Edward I contributed towards the building costs. It was closed in 1538 during the Dissolution of the Monasteries, but not demolished until the 19th century. Only modest remains survive today.

Continue to the end of Riverside, and turn up to a junction. Go left to reach the main road bridge spanning the Severn.

BRIDGNORTH

Timber-framed buildings, Bridgnorth

The most dramatic of the Severnside towns, Bridgnorth is unlike anywhere else in Britain and comes as a surprise when you arrive here for the first time because of the way it gathers at the top of a sandstone cliff.

It was in 912 that King Alfred's daughter, Ethelfleda, built a fortified township above the Severn, a township that was later to grow into the Bridgnorth we know today. Built at a strategic position, and a centre of communications, a river crossing and a port, it was almost inevitable that Bridgnorth would prosper. By the 13th century, the only Shropshire town greater in importance was Shrewsbury, although Bridgnorth was a much busier port, one of the busiest in Europe. There were three dockyards in the town, where numerous boats were built, while as a flourishing port Bridgnorth naturally attracted industry, particularly ironworks and carpet mills, as well as brewing, tanning and a variety of other trades.

Like many parts of Britain, by the 19th century, Bridgnorth was declining as an industrial centre, and the opening in 1862 of the Severn Valley Railway, linking Shrewsbury with Worcester, heralded the end for river trade. Only a century later the railway was itself closed, but a preservation society was formed and steam trains now run regularly between Bridgnorth and Kidderminster, contributing significantly to the tourist trade that is a vital part of Bridgnorth's economy today. Nowadays, the Severn, clear and unpolluted, is a haven for anglers, walkers and wildlife; at the height of summer it is not unusual to see the river carpeted with water crowfoot.

Bridgnorth is actually two towns: High Town, which crowns the sandstone cliff, and Low Town, which occupies the riverside below and the east bank. A road links the two, with further pedestrian access provided by seven ancient stairways and the ancient Cartway, one of Shropshire's most interesting streets. A remarkable cliff railway, opened in 1892 and now the only inland cliff railway in Britain, provides an alternative route. The oldest and steepest inland funicular railway in England makes the journey at least 150 times a day.

Low Town tends to be neglected by visitors, but is full of interest, with charming buildings and a good view of High Town from the bridge spanning the Severn. But it is High Town that has the most to offer, including the remains of a castle, built by Robert de Belleme, the son of Roger de Montgomery, in 1101–1102, although the keep was built by Henry II about 60 years later. The castle was surrendered by its Royalist garrison to Cromwell in 1646 during the Civil War, and subsequently dismantled. All that remains is the keep, tilted at a crazy angle three times greater than the Leaning Tower of Pisa. The medieval Northgate, which houses the Northgate Museum, stands guard at one end of the High Street while the Italianate splendour of the New Market Buildings, with its Childhood and Costume Museum, stands at the other.

Castle Walk provides a fine view; in fact, Charles I called it the finest in his kingdom. Neighbouring East Castle Street is one of Bridgnorth's most elegant thoroughfares, with gracious Georgian buildings leading the eye to the neo-Classical church of St Mary Magdalene, built in 1792 to the design of Thomas Telford.

The original parish church is St Leonard's, at the other end of town, a commanding edifice of dark red sandstone, which stands in a calm little oasis of period buildings. Steps descend from the church to the river, but of the ancient staircases and passageways linking the cliff-top with the riverside it is Cartway that is the best known. For centuries it was the main route out of High Town, and today it is still lined with attractive buildings, most notable of which is the gabled, timber-framed Bishop Percy's House, dated 1580. Several of Cartway's houses have heavy wooden shutters, designed for protection from the jostling of carts, wagons and horses. There are caves in the sandstone, which were used as homes until 1856, and there are more by the riverside, formerly used for storage as well as habitation.

The Severn Way

Other highlights of Bridgnorth include the former Town Hall (1650–1652), Waterloo Terrace, Stoneway Steps and the railway station, now the northern terminus of the Severn Valley Railway. Like most Shropshire towns, however, its greatest charm lies in its harmonious and unpretentious mix of architectural styles, best appreciated in a leisurely walk around its endlessly fascinating streets.

STAGE 12
Bridgnorth to Upper Arley

Start	Bridgnorth
Finish	Upper Arley
Distance	16.5km (10¼ miles)
Ascent	165m (550ft)
Descent	180m (600ft)

Between Bridgnorth and Hampton the Severn Way simply follows the river, mainly through waterside meadows. This is agreeable walking, with the Severn Valley Railway for company: the railway stations at Bridgnorth and Hampton are well worth a visit.

At the bridge, cross the road and descend to a paved area, which can be very slippery when wet. Go forward onto a narrow gravel path at the riverside, that later moves into riverside fields, with steep, tree-clad cliffs rising to your right. In recent years, many more trees, including wild cherries, have been planted at the foot of the cliffs. The river, however, is bordered mainly by alders and willows, trees that are tolerant of flooding.

The route passes beneath the **A458**. Further on, the Way briefly comes out to the **B4555**, opposite **Daniels Mill**. Turn left and walk beside the road until, opposite The Knowle, you can leave the road and turn through a metal kissing-gate to walk down beside a fence to rejoin

STAGE 12 – BRIDGNORTH TO UPPER ARLEY

QUATFORD

Quatford is one of the oldest settlements in the area, being listed in the Domesday Book. This was once the site of a camp established by Danish invaders in 893, and the Norman Earl of Shrewsbury, Roger de Montgomery, later built a settlement on the site in the 1070s. Quatford was settled because of the ease of fording the River Severn. Its name came from it being a ford near Quatt. As the River Severn became deeper, a bridge was built at the site instead. In the 11th century, a small castle was built on high ground overlooking the river, but was demolished a few years later. The earthworks of the castle still stand by the river and some Norman work survives in the church.

Quatford's importance as a crossing of the River Severn was diminished when another bridge, at a better defended site, was built two miles upstream; here, a settlement was formed at the 'bridge north of Quatford', now known as Bridgnorth, which became the major town in the district.

the original route back at the river's edge, at another kissing-gate. Now simply continue parallel to the river.

When the path meets buildings and a surfaced lane at **Lower Forge** – the site of a former ironworks that specialised in nail-making – keep left, and almost immediately branch left to a narrow riverside path. Stay beside the river once more, and after crossing a tributary, Mor Brook, at a narrow bridge, the route runs close to the course of the **Severn Valley Railway**, and will now offer numerous opportunities to see the splendid locomotives that operate on this popular line.

Hampton Station (Severn Valley Railway)

THE SEVERN WAY

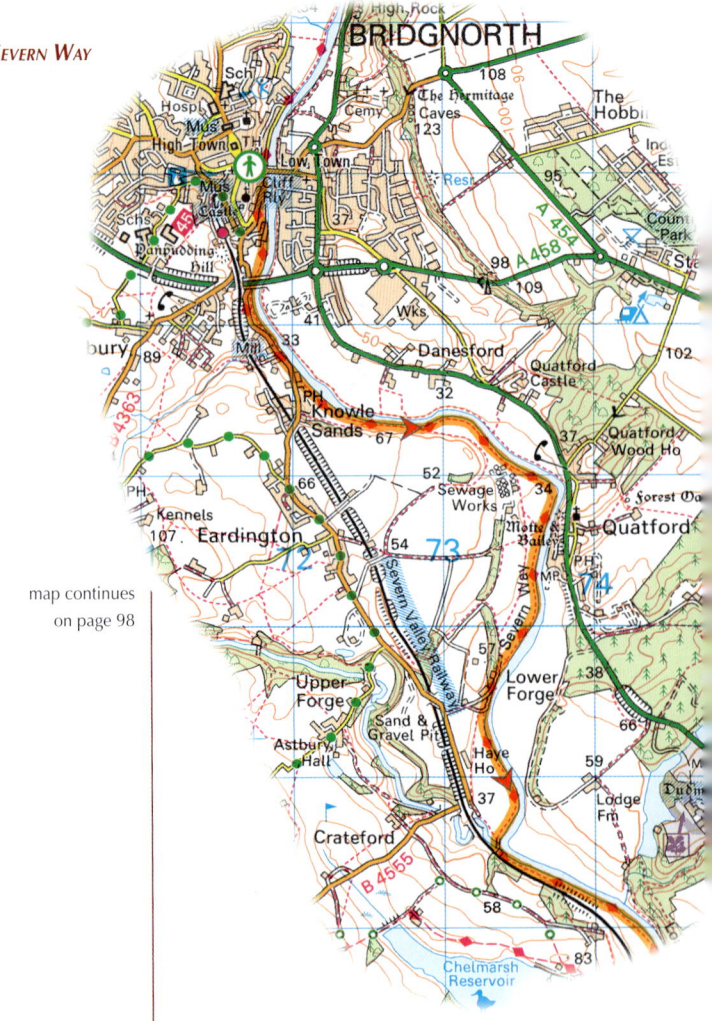

map continues on page 98

The **Severn Valley Railway** (SVR) is arguably the most popular preserved line in the country, and uses a large number of beautifully restored locomotives and carriages operating on a delightful route between Bridgnorth and Kidderminster. Trains run

STAGE 12 – BRIDGNORTH TO UPPER ARLEY

throughout the year although to a much-reduced timetable in winter. From May to October, however, there are frequent services and the line is probably busier now than at any time in its history (**www.svr.co.uk**).

Easy walking along the edge of riverside pastures leads past the grounds of **Dudmaston Hall** on the far bank, although it is the birdlife on the river that is most likely to command your attention.

The **Dudmaston Estate** has remained in the same family for 850 years, although it was given to the National Trust in 1978. Dudmaston provides a classical setting for a collection of modern and contemporary art. The modern art galleries were assembled by diplomat Sir George Labouchere, while his wife Rachel showed off her collections of botanical drawings and watercolours.

Soon after leaving Dudmaston behind, a waterworks footbridge (no public access) looms ahead, beyond which the Way goes swiftly on to **Hampton**, where

Mercian Way milepost (cycle route)

HAMPTON

The village comprises just a few cottages, chalets and caravans. The station, however, merits a detour. Great wicker baskets of damsons used to be loaded onto the trains here and transported to Manchester to be made into dye for the cotton trade. Those days are long gone, but something of their atmosphere remains, and not surprisingly Hampton Station has featured in many period films and TV programmes. Across the river is Hampton Loade; the second part of its name derives from a Saxon word for ford. From 1796 until 1866, there were forges at Hampton Loade where Papermill Brook joins the Severn, but today it is a popular spot with anglers, walkers and picnickers.

The Severn crossing at this point has been in use for around 400 years, and may have provided a route across the Severn during the Middle Ages. In 2004, a new ferry was built by the Ironbridge Gorge Museum to the design

THE SEVERN WAY

of the previous boat, which had seen 38 years' service. The new craft is of wooden construction, measures 20ft by 9ft, and carries up to 12 passengers.

Hampton Loade Ferry is a pedestrian cable ferry, known as a reaction ferry, propelled by the river current. An overhead cable is suspended across the river, and the ferry is tethered by a second cable to a pulley block that runs on the suspended cable. To operate the ferry it is angled into the current, causing the current to move it across the river (http://hamptonloadeferry.webs.com).

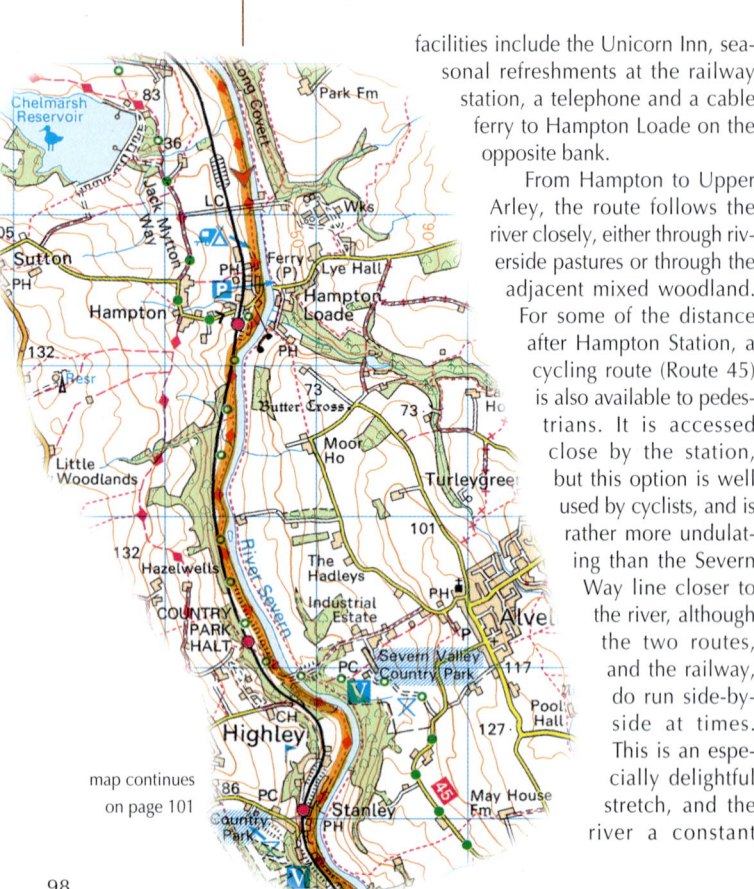

facilities include the Unicorn Inn, seasonal refreshments at the railway station, a telephone and a cable ferry to Hampton Loade on the opposite bank.

From Hampton to Upper Arley, the route follows the river closely, either through riverside pastures or through the adjacent mixed woodland. For some of the distance after Hampton Station, a cycling route (Route 45) is also available to pedestrians. It is accessed close by the station, but this option is well used by cyclists, and is rather more undulating than the Severn Way line closer to the river, although the two routes, and the railway, do run side-by-side at times. This is an especially delightful stretch, and the river a constant host to a variety of birdlife, including goosander, pochard, Canada goose, common sandpiper and mallard.

Having passed the ferry, bear left towards the river and enter a large riverside field. The Way now continues pleasantly to reach the Severn Valley Country Park, on the edge of **Highley**.

> The award-winning 51-hectare **Severn Valley Country Park** straddles the river, including land at both Highley (west bank) and Alveley (east bank), linked by a footbridge, the Miners' Bridge.
>
> Both Highley and Alveley are former mining and quarrying centres at the northern extreme of the Wyre Forest coalfield. Quarrying, in particular, has a long history here; it is believed that some of the stone for Worcester Cathedral came from Highley, sent downstream by boat. Coal mining began in the Middle Ages, but remained small-scale until the 19th century. Miners' Bridge was built both for the convenience of the workers and to bring coal from the east bank to the railway on the west bank.
>
> Production switched to the Alveley Colliery in 1936, which at its peak employed 1000 men and produced some 300,000 tonnes of coal a year. Mining ceased in 1969 and the area was badly scarred by spoil heaps. In 1986 a reclamation scheme began, and in 1992 Severn Valley Country Park opened. It is now managed by Shropshire Council and attracts around 90,000 visitors a year.
>
> The nearby village of Alveley has attractive cottages, a 12th-century church, and what is claimed to be Shropshire's oldest pub.

When you reach the Miners' Bridge, you can either go forward beneath the bridge, or up steps to access Highley (pubs and shops). The village is about 10 minutes' walk away, but contains little to justify the diversion other than a Norman church and an adjacent timber-framed house. The riverside path continues to a small settlement, **Stanley**, next to Highley Station, only a short distance from the riverside.

THE SEVERN WAY

Beside the Severn, on the way to Upper Arley

STANLEY AND HIGHLEY STATION

Stanley was a busy place for centuries, long before the railway was built, with barge traffic carrying coal, stone and timber. The Ship Inn was licensed in 1770, and originally catered for bargees, miners and quarrymen. Today, it's popular with walkers, anglers and railway enthusiasts. For many of the latter, Highley Station is the finest on the SVR, with its evocative ticket office and waiting room and flower-filled platform. The station opened to the public on 1 February 1862 and closed on 8 September 1963 when through passenger services to Shrewsbury ceased after 101 years.

This was formerly a very important transport hub of a colliery district, with four coal mines nearby, all linked by standard and narrow gauge branch lines, cable inclines and aerial ropeways to the Severn Valley line.

Highley's original footbridge had to be demolished in the early 1970s for safety reasons but a new footbridge was opened in 2009. The station, like many other stations, has won awards for its restoration and continuing level of appearance, but Highley is unique in its atmosphere and authenticity, and has also been used for television and film locations.

STAGE 12 – BRIDGNORTH TO UPPER ARLEY

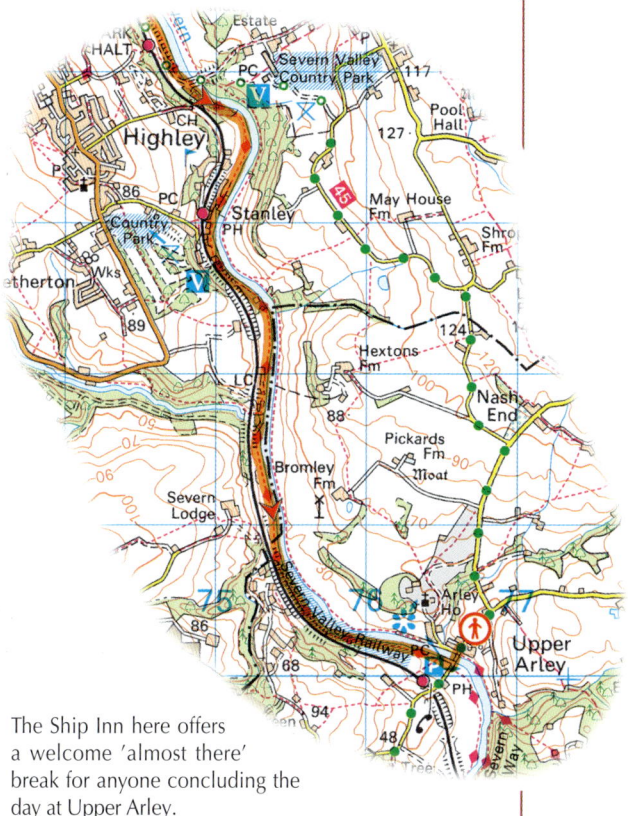

The Ship Inn here offers a welcome 'almost there' break for anyone concluding the day at Upper Arley.

The Severn Way goes on past Stanley as a broad, rough-surfaced track. When you reach a junction, turn left on a descending gravel track back to the riverside.

Delightful walking between river and railway now leads towards **Upper Arley**, the first Worcestershire village on the Way, where the river is crossed on a pedestrian bridge.

WORCESTERSHIRE

Diglis Locks, near Worcester

WORCESTERSHIRE

A mistletoe-decked tree on the way to Upton-on-Severn

The stretch of the Way through Worcestershire does have a number of minor undulations, but apart from a slight deviation at Grimley, is never far from the river. As a result, this section tends to be the worst affected by riverside mud. The countryside is outstanding, but progress by the river can be tiring. Here, the river has widened and generally makes slow progress, but there is plenty of evidence along the route to tell of its latent power.

THE SEVERN WAY

STAGE 13
Upper Arley to Stourport-on-Severn

Start	Upper Arley
Finish	Stourport-on-Severn
Distance	11.9km (7½ miles)
Ascent	135m (440ft)
Descent	140m (460ft)

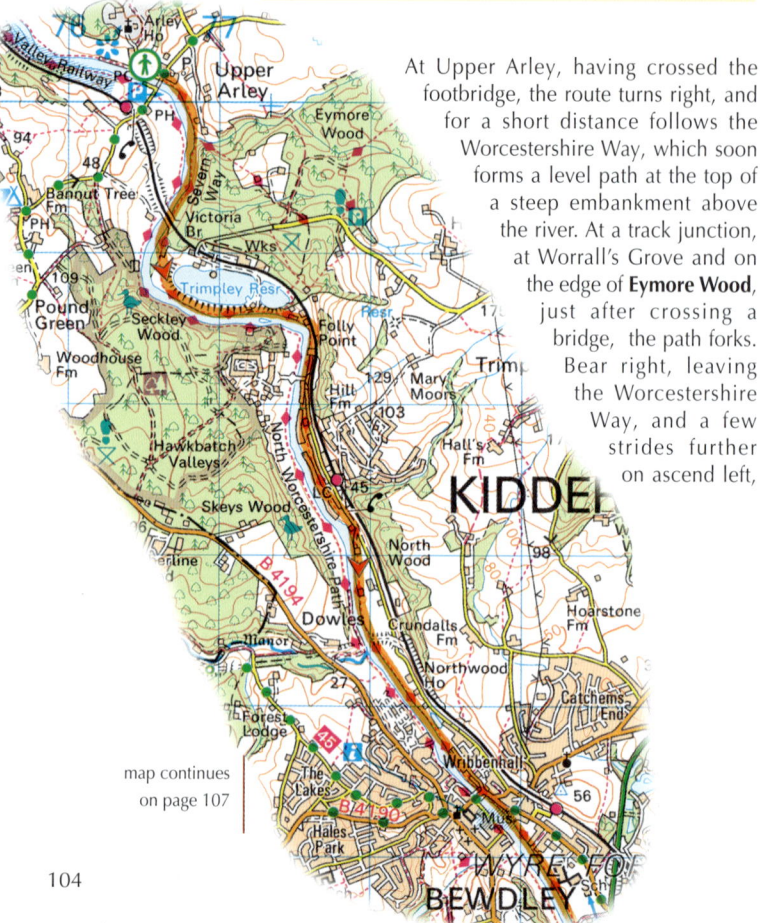

At Upper Arley, having crossed the footbridge, the route turns right, and for a short distance follows the Worcestershire Way, which soon forms a level path at the top of a steep embankment above the river. At a track junction, at Worrall's Grove and on the edge of **Eymore Wood**, just after crossing a bridge, the path forks. Bear right, leaving the Worcestershire Way, and a few strides further on ascend left,

map continues on page 107

STAGE 13 – UPPER ARLEY TO STOURPORT-ON-SEVERN

Approaching the footbridge at Upper Arley

then descend right, on a wide track through the edge of Eymore Wood.

> This is the easternmost extension of **Wyre Forest**, and although it was turned into a plantation, most of the trees are European larch, which make for lighter, more open woodland, and are a delight, especially in autumn. There have been trees growing here for over 10,000 years, and some authorities think that people have been living in the area for the same period, coupled with evidence that the Romans settled in the area. Wyre was for a time a Royal Forest, used as a royal chase for hunting.

When the track forks, stay by the river to pass **Victoria Bridge**, designed by John Fowler, the engineer responsible for the original London Underground. The bridge featured in the 1978 remake of John Buchan's *The Thirty-nine Steps*, starring Robert Powell. Beyond Victoria Bridge and Eymore Wood, the Way breaks out into an open meadow immediately adjacent to **Trimpley Reservoirs**, constructed in 1968 to supplement the Elan Valley water supply to Birmingham.

Leave the reservoir grounds at a metal gate, continuing through riverside scrub and mixed woodland, to a broad stony track at a car park adjoining the Elan Aqueduct. Continue beyond the aqueduct onto a narrow, surfaced lane. Continue following the lane a little further, but keep an eye open for a waymarked metal gate on the right, giving into rough pasture, passing close by an isolated house, and across a number of riverside meadows, the route linked by a series of metal gates. A broad track leads on past the abutments of an old railway (Dowles Bridge), and continues easily, with the houses of Bewdley coming into view ahead. The Way approaches Bewdley through a small urban park at the riverside. On the far side, keep forward where the surfaced path bends left to a gate beyond which the route is deflected around the rowing club to rejoin the path from the park. Keep forward along a surfaced lane to the bridge into **Bewdley**.

BEWDLEY

Bewdley was given to the Norman baron Roger Mortimer soon after the Conquest, and for a time was the administrative centre for the Council in the Marches of Wales. It made good use of its position on the Severn to engage in trade, gradually developing as a major river port. Goods coming upstream from Bristol were distributed throughout the Midlands and Bewdley's own trade goods met with a ready market downstream. Its early prosperity is reflected in the splendid buildings lining the narrow, winding streets and the long, straight waterfront, the finest in the Midlands. Many of its houses were given new façades in the 18th century, so Bewdley has the air of a Georgian town built to a medieval street plan.

The town has a varied range of pubs, restaurants, tea rooms and shops. Bewdley Station is the headquarters of the Severn Valley Railway.

At the river bridge either cross the road (but not the bridge) and go forward, or turn right to go down steps and pass under the bridge into a formal grassed area. In the latter case, follow the path out to rejoin the road, and turn right.

The route soon goes ahead into Stourport Road. Where it bends left, leave it, on the right, to cross in front of houses and continue on a riverside path, which later runs along the edge of a large playing field. Keep on and pass

Stage 13 – Upper Arley to Stourport-on-Severn

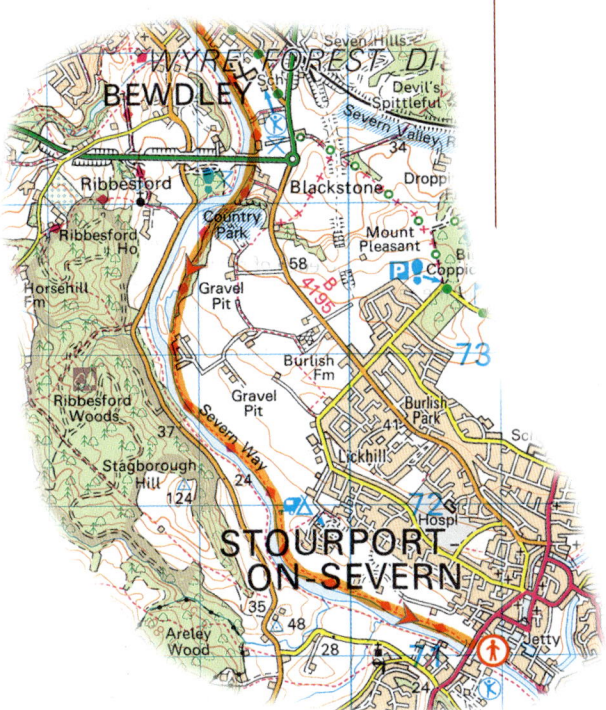

beneath the Bewdley bypass and on to a track junction below the prominent **Blackstone Rock**.

The rock has a number of **caves** which are believed to have once provided shelter for hermits, and may well have provided temporary shelter for travellers prevented by high water from crossing the river to reach Bewdley in the days before its bridge was built.

At the track junction, bear right through a metal gate. The track eventually climbs up to pass through a

THE SEVERN WAY

sandstone cutting. On the other side, descend, but when the track swings right, towards the river, leave it by going forward on a field path below a steep wooded cliff.

On the far bank of the Severn stands **Ribbesford House**, which during World War 2 housed officers of the Free French Forces under General de Gaulle.

Keep an eye open for a stile on the left that takes the path into the edge of mixed woodland, and press on in the same direction across bracken slopes and on past a shallow pond and water-logged meadows. Eventually, the track leads round into Severn Bank Park, then continues as a riverside path above a low bank. In due course, the path feeds into the grounds of the Stourport Motor Yacht and Bungalow Association, beyond which it continues as a broad track. The track, at a gate, gives onto a surfaced track parallel with the river and running along the edge of a large park.

The riverside path finally leads under an arched bridge on the edge of **Stourport**.

The Angel pub at Stourport

STAGE 14
Stourport-on-Severn to Worcester

Start	Stourport-on-Severn
Finish	Worcester
Distance	20.5km (12¾ miles)
Ascent	160m (520ft)
Descent	165m (540ft)

STOURPORT-ON-SEVERN

Stourport-on-Severn is uniquely the only town in Britain built solely as a consequence of the coming of the canals, in this instance the Staffordshire and Worcestershire Canal, opened in 1771. Originally, it was intended that the canal would join the River Severn at Bewdley, but that idea was rejected, and instead attention focused on a small hamlet called Lower Mitton. Two black-and-white houses from around the end of the 16th century still exist, on Mitton Street.

Popular legend has it that Derbyshire-born engineer James Brindley, one of the most notable engineers of the 18th century, chose Lower Mitton over Bewdley for his canal because the citizens of Bewdley did not want his 'stinking ditch' passing through their town. In fact, Lower Mitton, Stourport as it was to become, made more sense: a canal joining the Severn at Bewdley would have had to cross several hills. But by joining at Stourport it could follow the Stour valley, a prospect that was economically much more viable.

The Staffordshire and Worcestershire Canal linked the Severn with the Trent and Mersey and as a result Stourport became the busiest inland port in the Midlands after Birmingham. The town rapidly expanded and by the 1780s there were brass and iron foundries, a vinegar works, tan yards, worsted spinning mills, carpet mills, barge and boat building yards, warehouses, shops, houses and inns.

Leave Stourport on a riverside track passing the entrance to the amusement park, and go on to the lock system of Stourport Basin. Cross the locks and head for the Tontine Inn. Press on to pass the Angel pub, just before crossing the **River Stour** at its confluence with the Severn. The path now goes on to run along the edge of an open field and later passes a row of riverfront cottages.

THE SEVERN WAY

On the opposite bank stands **Redstone Rock.** Like many sandstone cliffs in this area, it is riddled with caves, many of which were inhabited by hermits, who, in this instance, may have manned the former ferry at Redstone Crossing, an ancient river crossing first recorded in the 13th century.

map continues on page 113

STAGE 14 – STOURPORT-ON-SEVERN TO WORCESTER

The Way runs on to reach a large boatyard; bear left into this, but soon swing round back towards the river, and then keep on to pass **Stourport Marina**, and, further on, Lincomb Weir, and then Lincomb Locks, the northernmost locks on the river.

The route moves on to pass another caravan site, one of many along the Severn, beyond which a path leads to a footbridge and on into light woodland before reaching yet another caravan park. The route now treads lightly along riverside pastures, many in number, all of them offering peaceful rambling, before reaching Holt Lock. A short way further on an A-road is carried over the Severn; approach this by going round Riverside House and up steps to the bridge. Cross the bridge, and, on the other side, turn left to pass in front of Holt Fleet Hotel.

Cross a small parking area to a gate, immediately after which the path climbs steeply into the edge of woodland, then follows a level path to a stile into a sloping pasture. Bear right, following a broad track up to a gate and stile, beyond which join a concrete farm track and follow this to the village of **Holt**, something of a treasure in a quiet, unobtrusive way.

Leaving Stourport, bound for Worcester

The Severn Way

HOLT

There has been a settlement at Holt since Saxon times, when a village developed around the castle and church. The manor of Holt was granted to Urso D'Abitot who built the original castle. After his death, the manor passed to Walter de Beauchamp, who had married Urso's daughter. The name Holt comes from a Saxon word meaning 'wood'. The location was well chosen for its defensive position against Welsh marauders.

On the left is Holt Castle. The 14th-century tower, built by Lord Beauchamp, is a relic of an embattled castle that is now complemented by a 15th-century manor house. Opposite is St Martin's Church, with a fine lychgate. The church is believed to date from the 11th century, and is one of the finest Norman churches in Worcestershire.

Nothing remains of the original buildings of the village, which were made from perishable materials, nor is there any documentation to confirm when the church was built. The Domesday Book records that the village had a population of 12 villeins (the highest grade of peasant bound to the lord and farming about 15 acres of land) and 24 bordars (a lower order of peasant).

Keep on past Holt's architectural splendours and, at Holt Grange, where the road bends to the right, keep forward on a descending surfaced lane towards a small industrial unit on the left. Maintain the same direction past this, now on a rising gravel track from the top of which (at a gate) go forward (across a large field sometimes used as a caravan site) to a distant caravan and mobile home retail park. Enter this at a metal gate and walk through the area to the far side.

Now go through a gate onto a descending track to a T-junction. Here, turn right for a few strides, and then left still following a broad track until it meets a surfaced lane at a bend. Keep on in the same direction and then, just after crossing a stream the ongoing track divides. Bear left briefly and then swing right to cross what used to be a sizeable working quarry, of which nothing now remains. The objective is the first of a stretch of overhead powerlines and with the tower of Grimley church beyond.

On reaching the first powerline go through a metal field gate and follow a track into a field and up a slight

STAGE 14 – STOURPORT-ON-SEVERN TO WORCESTER

rise to a stile in a field corner. Keep forward along the field edge, but then, halfway around the second side of the field, pass through a gate into the grounds of St Bartholomew's church at **Grimley**. The church is believed to be 12th century in origin, but rebuilt in the 19th century.

Walk through the churchyard to emerge down steps into the village lane. Turn left and pass the Wagon Wheel

map continues on page 114

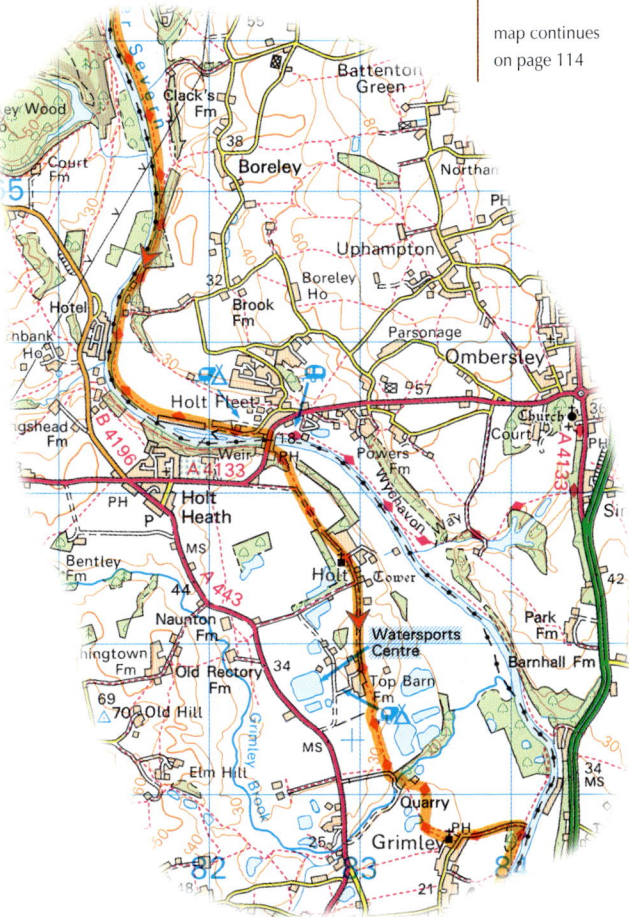

THE SEVERN WAY

pub, then follow a broad track down to rejoin the River Severn. Before long, the route passes **Bevere Island** and its nearby lock.

Bevere Island is the second largest of all the natural islets in the River Severn and used to be a refuge for the citizens of the area. It was here they came to escape Danish raiders in 1041, and here too they tried to flee the plague in 1637. As a result, the island was often referred to as The Camp. An iron footbridge connects Bevere Island to the east bank and a lock, built in 1844, to the west bank. The name comes from Beaver Island, but the beavers died out over 1000 years ago.

Easy walking leads on to the ever-so-convenient Camp House pub, licensed by Cromwell after the

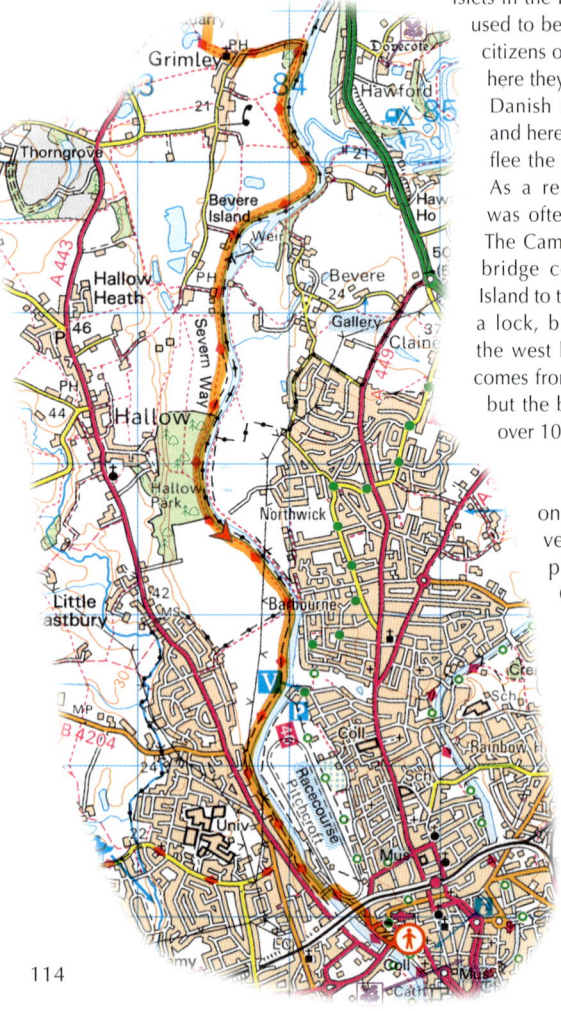

STAGE 14 – STOURPORT-ON-SEVERN TO WORCESTER

Battle of Worcester (1651). On reaching the pub, turn right on a narrow path, then go left at the rear of the pub and across a small paddock, bearing left on the far side to rejoin the river.

Between Camp House and Worcester, the Way never leaves the riverside, and for a long stretch passes through woodland that screens the buildings of Worcester from view. Eventually, however, the outskirts of the city intrude, and finally the path leads on below houses perched precariously, it seems, above the river, or set back a short distance. The path emerges at Henwick Parade, a raised, surfaced track that leads on to a footbridge (Sabrina Bridge) over the Severn, opened in 1992. Cross here, and turn right on the other side to pass below the railway viaduct to reach Worcester Bridge.

Farm fields on the approach to Worcester

The Severn Way

STAGE 15
Worcester to Upton-upon-Severn

Start	Worcester
Finish	Upton-upon-Severn
Distance	19.3km (12 miles)
Ascent	110m (370ft)
Descent	110m (370ft)

Between Worcester and Upton-upon-Severn, the Way barely leaves the riverside. The former deviation around Clifton is now avoided by the simple expedient of sticking to the river flood embankment.

WORCESTER

Worcester is a fascinating place, with a pedigree that is more than 2000 years in the making, as numerous Iron Age finds demonstrate. It achieved a degree of prominence in Roman times, when an iron smelting industry flourished, and a port was established mainly to transport salt from mines at Droitwich.

Once the Romans had departed, the Saxons found the place to their liking, and Worcester became a political and religious centre. But it was under the Normans that the stature of Worcester grew; they built a castle and a cathedral, and it was at this time that the city received its Royal Charter from Richard I (the Lionheart), in 1189.

For hundreds of years, Worcester grew and prospered, making abundant use of the Severn for trade. With the exception of two civil wars, political life in and around Worcester was relatively calm. The first war was from 1135–1148, but it is the second (from 1642–1651) that is better known. It was in this second civil war that both the first and last battles took place close to Worcester. The city was staunchly loyal to the Stuart cause, which earned it the name 'The Faithful City' from Charles II (1660–1685). By the mid-17th century, Worcester was ranked 11th among the great cities of England, and continued to thrive, notably during the Georgian and Victorian periods.

The continuation takes the riverside 'promenade' that runs south from Worcester Bridge, passing below the cathedral. Continue past the Diglis Hotel, and ahead to the footbridge over Diglis Basin. Press on along a

STAGE 15 – WORCESTER TO UPTON-UPON-SEVERN

Barges on the river at Worcester

map continues on page 118

surfaced lane to Diglis Lock. Keep to the left of Diglis Bridge, and then go forward on a grassy path that moves on above the Severn through light woodland cover. Briefly, the Way is diverted past a collapsing section by going left up steps and then back down again a short way further on.

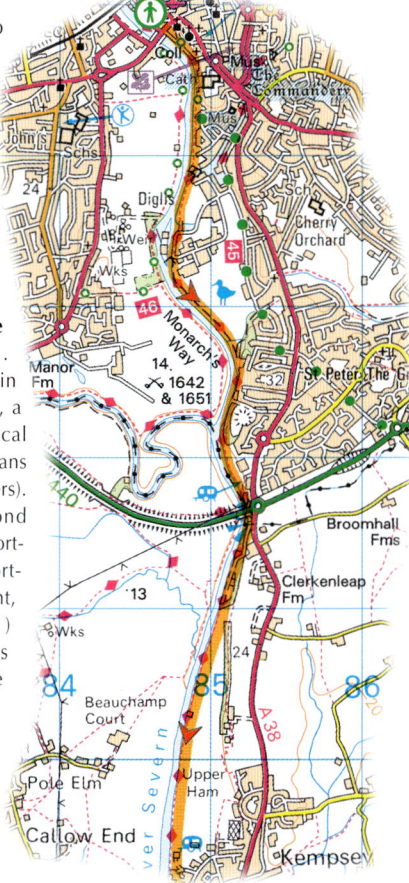

> Across the river, just north of its confluence with the River Teme, is one of the sites on which the **Battle of Worcester** was fought in 1651. This was the culminating episode in the English Civil War (1642–1651), a series of armed conflicts and political manoeuvring between Parliamentarians (Roundheads) and Royalists (Cavaliers). The first (1642–1646) and second (1648–1649) civil wars set the supporters of Charles I against the supporters of the so-called Long Parliament, while the third war (1649–1651) saw fighting between supporters of Charles II and supporters of the Rump Parliament that followed. The Civil War ended with Parliamentary victory at the Battle of Worcester on 3 September 1651.

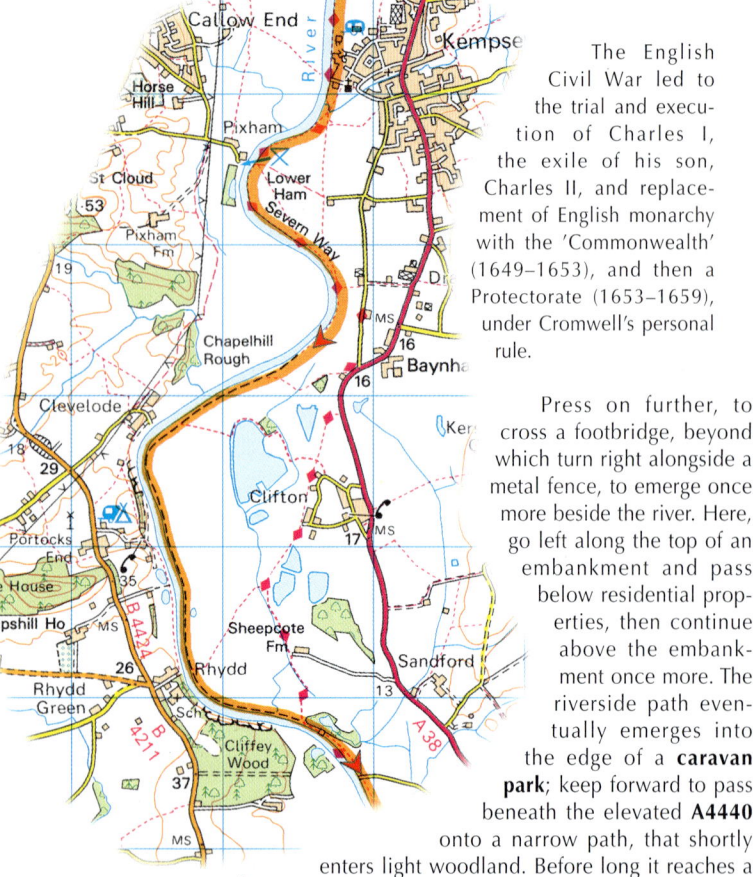

The English Civil War led to the trial and execution of Charles I, the exile of his son, Charles II, and replacement of English monarchy with the 'Commonwealth' (1649–1653), and then a Protectorate (1653–1659), under Cromwell's personal rule.

Press on further, to cross a footbridge, beyond which turn right alongside a metal fence, to emerge once more beside the river. Here, go left along the top of an embankment and pass below residential properties, then continue above the embankment once more. The riverside path eventually emerges into the edge of a **caravan park**; keep forward to pass beneath the elevated **A4440** onto a narrow path, that shortly enters light woodland. Before long it reaches a stretch of riverside moorings, on the far side of which a gate gives onto a large arable pasture at **Upper Ham**, and another caravan site on the outskirts of **Kempsey**, one of the county's oldest villages, and the site of Iron Age and Roman settlements.

The route takes a great loop around the edge of **Lower Ham**, passing the site of the former Pixham ferry crossing. It was here that Simon de Montfort crossed the Severn on the way to defeat at the Battle of Evesham.

map continues on page 120

Riverside moorings at Upper Ham, near Kempsey

Simon de Montfort, 6th Earl of Leicester, 1st Earl of Chester (about 1208–1265), was an Anglo-Norman nobleman. He led the barons' rebellion against Henry III during the Second Barons' War of 1263–1264, and subsequently became de facto ruler of England. During his rule, de Montfort called the first directly elected parliament in medieval Europe, and is regarded as one of the progenitors of modern parliamentary democracy. After a rule of just over a year, de Montfort was killed by forces loyal to the king.

On the far side of Lower Ham, pass through a gate and keep forward along an embankment, always parallel with the river, which it joins not far from **Severn Stoke**. After that, with just a slight deviation to pass through a fenced enclosure, the route returns to the riverside, and follows this until cornered below the imposing house of **Severn Bank**, a Grade II listed building dating from the 17th century, but largely remodelled around 1830.

At the end of the field, cross a stile on the left, and then follow the field edge out, below Severn Bank, to join the **A38**. Turn right here and follow the road

THE SEVERN WAY

Severn Bank House, near Upton-upon-Severn

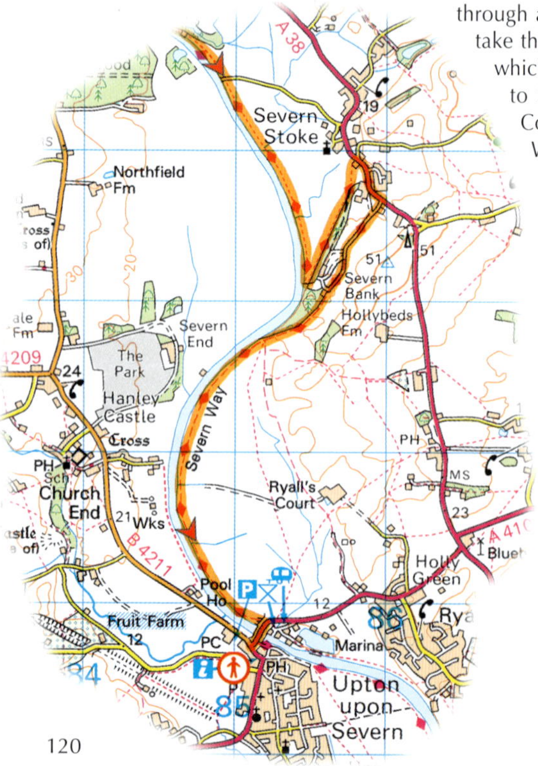

through a couple of bends, then take the first lane on the right, which leads past the entrance to Severn Bank, and then Coach House, where the Way bears left onto a grassy track, descending past Cliff Wood through a gate to rejoin the riverbank. Now simply follow the river towards **Upton**.

On reaching Upton Bridge, bear left through an underpass, doubling back on the other side to walk onto the bridge, going left towards the town centre.

STAGE 16

Upton-upon-Severn to Tewkesbury

Start	Upton-upon-Severn
Finish	Tewkesbury
Distance	11km (7 miles)
Ascent	25m (90ft)
Descent	25m (90ft)

This next section of the Way takes the route out of Worcestershire and into Gloucestershire, which it finally enters at Mythe Bridge, just north of Tewkesbury.

UPTON-UPON-SEVERN

Upton is a lovely, small town in the Malvern Hills District of Worcestershire, founded in 897. The town's bridge is the only one across the Severn between Worcester and Tewkesbury, other than the M50 motorway. The present bridge was built in 1940. Oliver Cromwell's soldiers crossed the Severn here before the Battle of Worcester. The town has a distinctive tower and copper-clad cupola known locally as the Pepperpot, the only surviving remnant of a former church.

Not surprisingly, Upton has always depended on the river for its prosperity. In the 13th century, the Bishop of Hereford used the town to land his supplies of wine here, and this and associated trade turned this modest town into a thriving port, handling timber, coal, salt, cider and bricks in its 18th-century heyday. Today, the town benefits from tourism, and stages a number of festivals each year that attract a wide audience.

Resume from Upton by turning down the cobbled lane that leads to the Plough Inn. Keep left at Bridge House, and pass the Swan Hotel, continuing along a concrete driveway to enter the corner of a large open pasture. Now simply keep forward along the field edge, parallel with the river.

The **large pasture**, Upper Ham, is a Site of Special Scientific Interest (SSSI), almost 60 hectares, and

THE SEVERN WAY

map continues
on page 124

designated for its rare, flower-rich grassland. This is a historic lammas meadow, so called because it was grazed from Lammas Day in August until early the next year. Plant species here include meadow sweet, meadow cranesbill, autumn crocus and narrow-leaved water dropwort, along with an interesting range of birds such as corn bunting, long-tailed tit, kestrel and redshank.

Upper Ham is also distinctive for its military features spanning a period from the mid-19th century to World War 2, which included a 1000-yard rifle range, and a brick-built target area from the 1860s, used regularly until 1925, and then by the Home Guard.

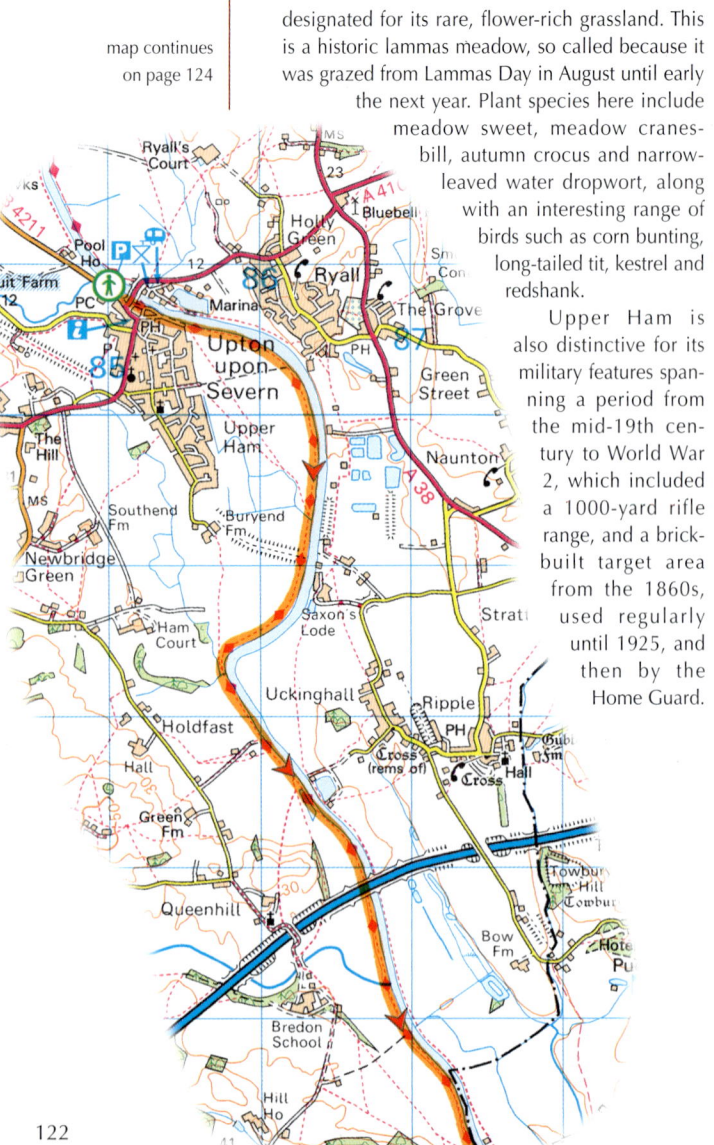

Easy riverside fields beside the Severn at Upton

Easy walking now ensues all the way to the outskirts of Tewkesbury. Not far south of the scattered village of **Holdfast** is Queenshill, a setting said to have inspired composer Edward Elgar, who was born on the outskirts of Worcester.

Pass on below the **M50**, beyond which the river forms the county boundary, the far bank now part of Gloucestershire. On that side, as Mythe Bridge is approached, a wooded cliff towers over the river, topped with the earthworks of a motte and bailey castle, known as Mythe Tute.

On reaching Mythe Bridge, cross a stile and shortly go left to join the **A438**. Stay on the left side of the road, to cross the bridge (and so pass into Gloucestershire), and go past traffic lights to the Alum House. Here, leave the road, turning left and going down gated steps. Keep left at the bottom and walk towards the river. There, turn left through an underpass, and then swing left over metal ladders onto a constructed pathway around **waterworks** buildings. The path leads to a pump house; here, cross more metal bridgework to emerge on the edge of a large meadow. Keep forward, riverside, to the confluence between the Severn and the Old Avon. Now follow the field edge round in a great loop, back towards Beaufort Bridge on the A38. Head towards the centre of **Tewkesbury**, but shortly descend steps on the right to follow the towpath alongside the Mill Avon.

THE SEVERN WAY

Borough Flour Mills buildings, Tewkesbury

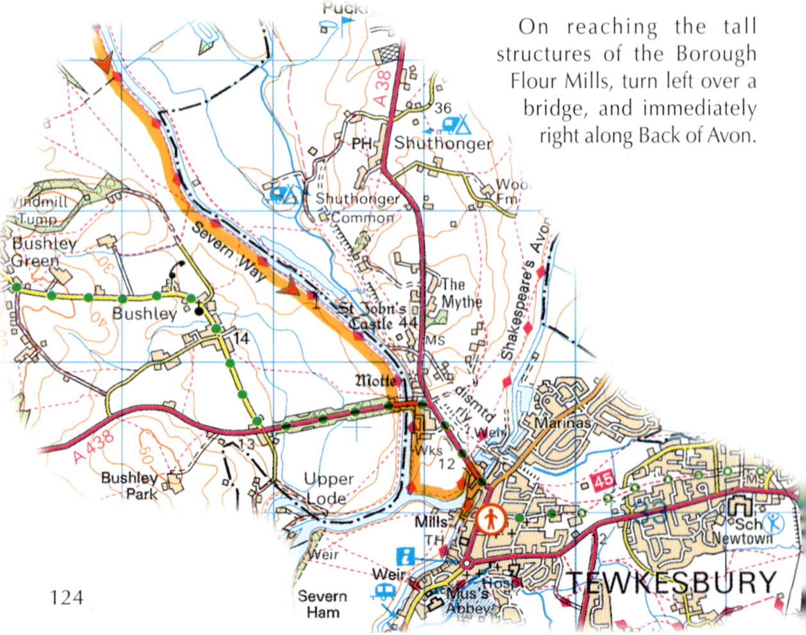

On reaching the tall structures of the Borough Flour Mills, turn left over a bridge, and immediately right along Back of Avon.

124

GLOUCESTERSHIRE

The Mill Avon, Tewkesbury

THE SEVERN WAY

Ancient oak, near Apperley

South of Tewkesbury, the Severn takes to meandering again, especially as it passes Gloucester city, after which it seems in no hurry to head for the sea. Here it is tidal, and the great Arlingham peninsula reveals low-tide sandbanks, the first real precursors of the estuary to come. Soon the Severn Sea, as it is known locally, brings an unmistakable maritime tang, the scent of seaweed and the hint of the distant Atlantic.

By the time it approaches the sea, the Severn is carrying a huge quantity of material eroded from its upper reaches, which goes to reinforce the mudflats of the massive estuary.

STAGE 17
Tewkesbury to Gloucester Docks

Start	Tewkesbury
Finish	Gloucester Docks
Distance	21.6km (13½ miles)
Ascent	125m (410ft)
Descent	125m (410ft)

TEWKESBURY

Tewkesbury is both a thriving town and a living museum of architecture and social history spanning more than 500 years. The town has such well-preserved medieval characteristics, with fine half-timbered Tudor buildings, overhanging upper-storeys and ornately carved doorways, that in 1964 the Council of British Archaeology listed it among 57 towns 'so splendid and so precious that the ultimate responsibility for them should be of national concern'.

The surrounding rivers and floodplain have effectively prevented the town from expanding, so that its long thin profile has scarcely altered since the Middle Ages. Most evidently, the town is dominated by the 12th-century abbey, a beautiful building with the highest Norman tower in England.

The name Tewkesbury comes from Theoc, the name of a Saxon who founded a hermitage here in the seventh century, and in the Old English tongue was called Theocsbury. Historically, Tewkesbury is a market town, serving a large rural area, and saw a degree of expansion in the period following World War 2. The town has also been a centre for flour milling for many centuries, and the water mill, the older Abbey Mill, still stands, although today converted for residential use. Until recently flour was milled at a more modern mill a short way upriver on the site of the town quay; parts of the mill date to 1865, when it was thought to be the largest and most modern flour mill in the world.

Go a short distance along Back of Avon to a footbridge spanning the river. On the other side, turn left onto a footpath that skirts **Severn Ham**.

> **Severn Ham** is an island of meadowland about 72 hectares (177 acres) between the Severn and the

THE SEVERN WAY

map continues on page 130

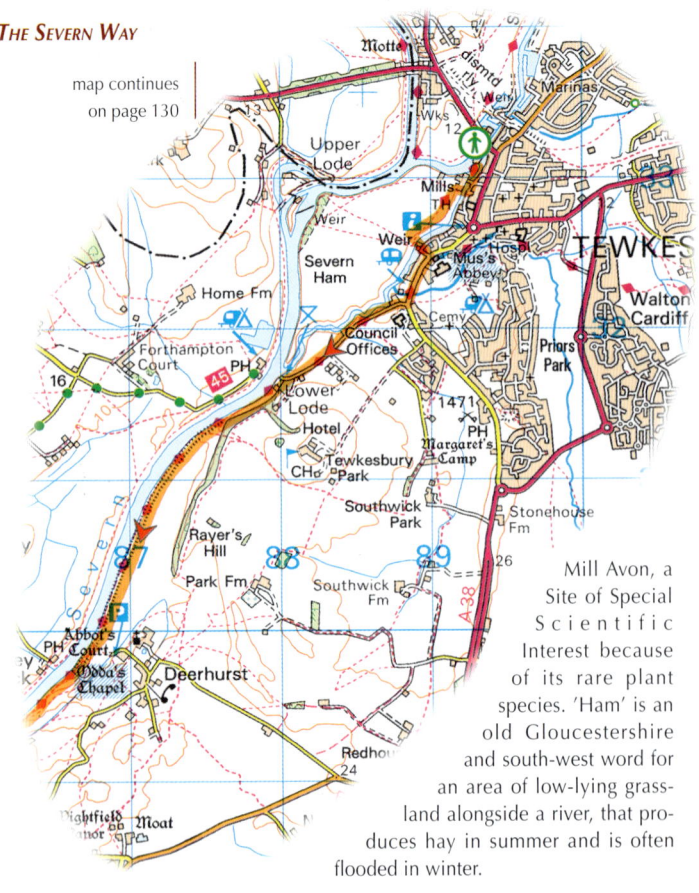

Mill Avon, a Site of Special Scientific Interest because of its rare plant species. 'Ham' is an old Gloucestershire and south-west word for an area of low-lying grassland alongside a river, that produces hay in summer and is often flooded in winter.

Recross the river at New Abbey Mills Sluice, by the **weir**, and then walk out along Mill Street to the main road at the Bell Hotel. Turn right and soon pass the former Tewkesbury Grammar School, founded in 1576 and housed for over 200 years in the abbey. Continue as far as Lower Lode Lane, and here turn right and follow a narrow lane to its end at a picnic site on the banks of the Severn.

New Abbey Mills Sluice, Tewkesbury

Along the lane, and diverting from it, the so-called **Battle Trail** leads to the 'Bloody Meadow', the site of the Battle of Tewkesbury on 4 May 1471. Here Edward IV's Yorkist forces defeated the House of Lancaster in a historic battle of the Wars of the Roses, with a bloody aftermath.

At the end of the lane, turn left past the Boathouse and then continue along the riverside path. Easy walking now leads on, passing **Deerhurst** and **Odda's Chapel**.

Odda's Chapel is one of the most complete surviving Saxon churches in England. Earl Odda had it built for the benefit of the soul of his brother Aelfric, who died on 22 December 1053. Ealdred, Bishop of Worcester consecrated it; an inscription dates the dedication to 12 April 1056. The chapel lay undiscovered for centuries, its walls hidden amidst the rambling rooms of a 17th-century farmhouse known as Abbot's Court. The nave had been made into a kitchen, while the chancel had become a bedroom. In 1865, the historic significance of the chapel was realised, and in 1885 it was disentangled from the farmhouse.

THE SEVERN WAY

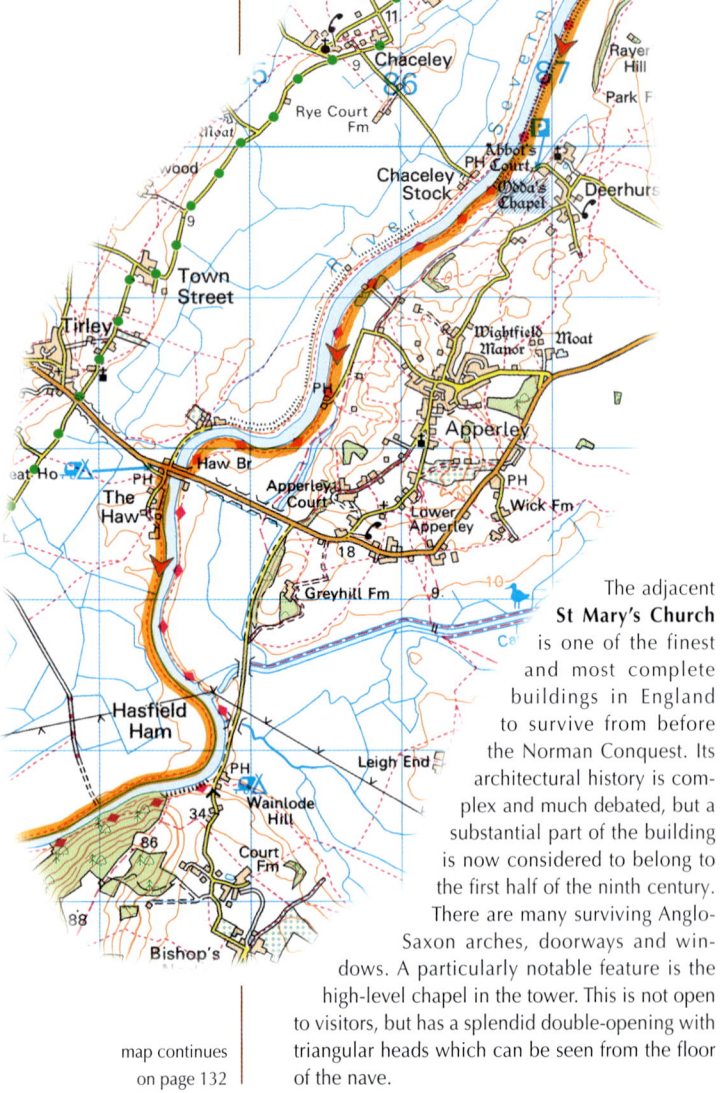

The adjacent **St Mary's Church** is one of the finest and most complete buildings in England to survive from before the Norman Conquest. Its architectural history is complex and much debated, but a substantial part of the building is now considered to belong to the first half of the ninth century. There are many surviving Anglo-Saxon arches, doorways and windows. A particularly notable feature is the high-level chapel in the tower. This is not open to visitors, but has a splendid double-opening with triangular heads which can be seen from the floor of the nave.

map continues on page 132

STAGE 17 – TEWKESBURY TO GLOUCESTER DOCKS

Gloucester Quay

Press on across a series of pleasant meadows, passing the Coalhouse Inn and forward through the Severnside Caravan Park to a stile, and then keep going easily to reach Haw Bridge. Here you pop out onto the B4213.

Cross the road and turn right to cross the bridge, opened in 1961 by the Duke of Beaufort, the Lord Lieutenant. Turn left down steps to pass in front of the former Haw Bridge Inn (now a private residence). Go forward through a metal stile/gate above the river and keep on along a raised embankment flanked by willow, roses, holly and honeysuckle.

Continue past a series of houses to a step-stile beside a gate, then continue on a broad track. Keep on past a final cottage and then resume the broad track. Soon pass into the Hasfield Estate, the route paralleling the river around the edge of Hasfield Ham, continuing easily towards the village of Ashleworth, reaching it at Ashleworth Quay, the oldest part of the village. An ancient ferry, which used to link Ashleworth Quay to Sandhurst on the east bank of the river, closed in the 1950s. Near the Quay is the former Boat Inn (closed), the ancient parish church of St Andrew and St Bartholomew, the Manor, the Court and the historic Tithe Barn (National Trust). The village centre, with its shop, bakery, tea room and post office is just over half a mile distant.

THE SEVERN WAY

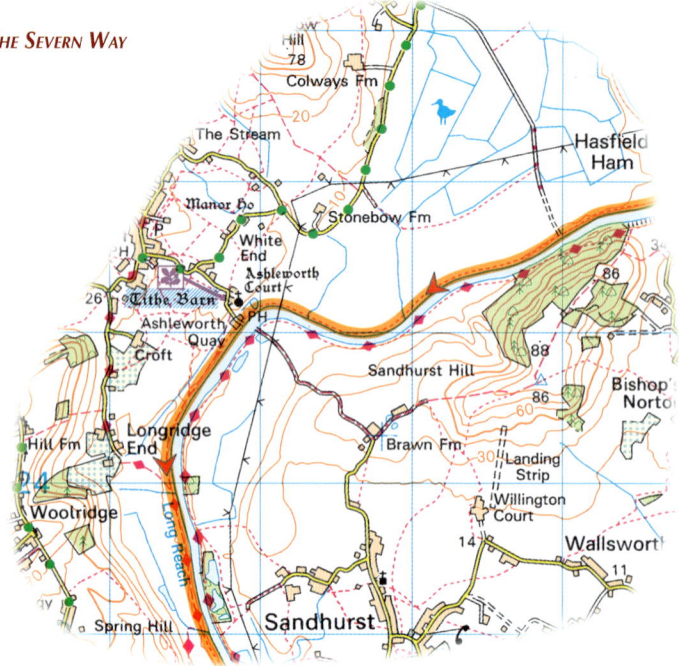

map continues
on page 134

Ashleworth Ham lies in the floodplains of the Severn Vale and is part of a much larger Site of Special Scientific Interest. The area floods easily, especially in winter, and as a result is a perfect wetland for overwintering wildfowl, large numbers of which are not uncommon, including as many as 4000 wigeon, 1500 teal and 1000 mallard along with smaller numbers of pintail, shoveler, tufted duck, pochard, goldeneye, great-crested and little grebe, Bewick and Whooper swans. In the summer months, there are breeding populations of lapwing, snipe, curlew, redshank, redstart, grasshopper warbler, sedge warbler, yellow wagtail and reed bunting.

From the Quay, go forward through a gate and then a couple of gated enclosures to reach the corner of an arable field. Now press on parallel with the river, eventually, after about 3km (2 miles) of easy walking, to reach Maisemore Park, where the river divides into the East and West Channels. The route now swings round to pass above a weir where it passes through two gates along a broad gravel track. The weir marks the upper limit of tidal flow on the Severn.

After the second gate, bear left and take to a field edge path leading to a step-stile close by a glorious row of poplars. Continue with the field edge path, walking out to reach a surfaced lane. Turn left and walk down to reach the A417 at the White Hart pub. The name, Maisemore, seems to be of Welsh origin, meaning 'great field' (Welsh: maes mawr).

At the A-road, turn left to cross Maisemore Bridge, which connects the village to Alney Island, and provides a viewpoint for the Severn Bore. Immediately over the bridge, turn left onto a broad track, and when this divides, bear right, and now walk along a direct track, part of the Three Choirs Way. Ignore the branching path taken by the Three Choirs Way and instead keep on to the far end of the track to Riverside Cottage. Here turn right, through a kissing-gate, to follow a field edge path that leads to another kissing-gate concealed in a corner

Gloucester cathedral

THE SEVERN WAY

that gives onto another arable field, now once more close to the river.

Keep following the field edge path as far as an obvious gap in the hedgerow on the left, just before overhead power lines. Turn through this and take to another field margin that leads round eventually to a kissing-gate just beneath the A40. The path continues beneath the A-road and curves round to another kissing-gate and then swings left to pass beneath a railway line at Town Ham.

Beyond the railway, pass through another gate to enter **Richard's Wood** of oak and ash, also known as **Alney Island Nature Reserve** planted in 1983 to commemorate the 500th anniversary of the charter given to Gloucester by Richard III. Continue on a broad track, and on the far side of the wood, pass through a gate. The ongoing path soon gives onto a surfaced section of an old road that leads out to a road junction.

Stage 17 – Tewkesbury to Gloucester Docks

Marina, Gloucester Docks

Go forward alongside the busy road as far as a branch on the left to a footpath for pedestrians and cyclists, signed for the city centre. This soon swings right under one of the carriageways and then takes to a pedestrian bridge spanning the river. On the other side, bear right to pass beneath the second carriageway and then as you pop out on the far side the cathedral in Gloucester appears directly ahead. Now go forward alongside a large traffic circulation known as The Island. On the far side of The Island, swing right with the road into The Quay. This is the point where anyone bound for the centre of the city can depart.

Keep right along The Quay, with the option of taking to a lower path alongside the quay, which further on needs to be quit for the roadside footpath.

Follow The Quay to Severn Road, just before Lock Warehouse, next to the locks, where this section of the walk ends. Anyone wanting to head for pubs, restaurants and shops should go forward onto the Riverside Walk and turn left at the marina, when the facilities will become obvious.

THE SEVERN WAY

GLOUCESTER

Elizabeth I granted Gloucester the formal status of a port with its own Custom House so that vessels trading with other countries could load and discharge their cargoes. The Custom House was used throughout the 17th century and the early part of the18th.

Evidence of Roman Quay walls were discovered in 1846 along with Saxon and Medieval quaysides along the old East Channel. In 1580, the quay, known then as the 'King's Quay' was designated the principal landing place in the new port of Gloucester. Construction of the second quay extending southwards was completed in 1623.

The cathedral in Gloucester is well worth the deviation, its foundation stone having been laid in 1089. The cathedral contains several funerary monuments including those of Robert Curthose (Robert II of Normandy), the eldest son of William the Conqueror and Edward II of England, the seventh Plantagenet king of England. The cathedral has featured in many TV and film productions including the first, second and sixth *Harry Potter* movies, *Doctor Who*, *Wolf Hall* and *Mary Queen of Scots*.

STAGE 18
Gloucester Docks to Upper Framilode

Start	Gloucester Docks
Finish	Upper Framilode
Distance	21km (13 miles)
Ascent	50m (165ft)
Descent	55m (180ft)

At the locks either cross the swing bridge and follow the road beyond, or cross the road to go forward a short distance towards the marina, and then take the footbridge on the right to pass alongside Lock Warehouse out to the road (turn left). Walk to a T-junction, and turn right up to the A38; there turn left and walk past the remains of **Llanthony Secunda Priory**.

STAGE 18 – GLOUCESTER DOCKS TO UPPER FRAMILODE

The **priory** is now nothing more than a group of evocative remains of a medieval priory of Augustinian Canons, still known as Secunda to distinguish it from the original Llanthony Priory Prima in Monmouthshire from where the first canons came.

By the 16th century, Llanthony Secunda was the sixth largest Augustinian house in England, in which a prior and 24 canons were attended by about 80 lay servants. It was also the richest, owning 97 churches and 51 well-appointed manors from Bedfordshire to Westmeath.

Cross the main road with care and turn into Sudmeadow Road, and keep an eye open for a footpath on the right (signposted) that runs between private gardens and a small industrial estate. At the end of the path, turn left to rejoin the East Channel of the Severn, and shortly resume flood-bank walking.

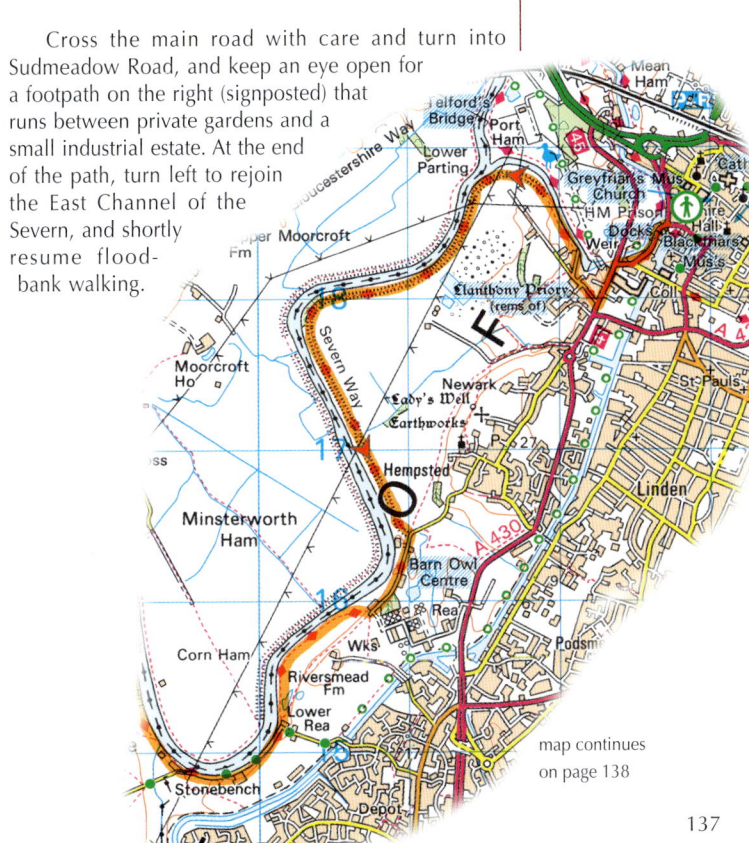

map continues on page 138

THE SEVERN WAY

Press on past a landfill site at Sud Meadow, and then keep on over two stiles, across riverside pastures.

On the approach to farm outbuildings, the route is diverted left from the floodbank across a field to a gate in a hedgerow, just after which cross a footbridge and join a lane. Turn right and follow the lane to its end at Severn Sound, and there go down a gravel path onto a grassy track to enter a large field, keeping right, near the Severn.

The Way eventually emerges onto a road at **Lower Rea** (Whitestones). Here, keep forward along the road (Elmore Lane West), taking care against approaching traffic, and continue as far as **Stonebench House**. Just before the entrance gates to the house, cross a stile on the right, passing the 'stone bench', and then follow the riverbank past the house, and on beyond to circle a narrow inlet. Now press on around the edge of an arable field, on the far corner of which the path leads to a stile and an ongoing path just above the river. Continue past Weir House, and then pick up the floodbanks, which are a familiar guide.

map continues on page 140

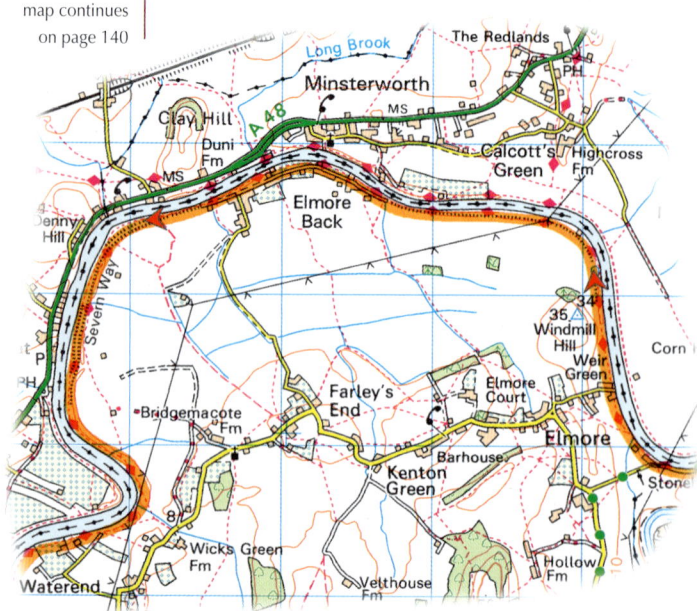

At Elmore Back

There is no mistaking the route, which parallels the river faithfully. The Severn has been tidal since Gloucester, and **Minsterworth**, on the opposite bank, is a popular place to watch the Severn Bore. There is a fine view of Minsterworth

SEVERN BORE

The Severn Bore is one of Britain's most spectacular natural phenomena, a surge wave of varying heights that can be seen in the estuary of the Severn, where the tidal range is the second highest in the world, being as much as 15m (50ft).

As many as 60 bores occur throughout the world where the river estuary is the right shape and the tidal conditions are such that the wave is able to form. The Severn Bore (one of eight in the UK) is one of the biggest in the world, and the shape of the river's estuary means that the water is funnelled into an increasingly narrow channel as the tide rises, forming a large wave. The river's course takes it past Avonmouth, where it is approximately 5 miles wide, then Beachley and Aust, Lydney and Sharpness, where the width has reduced to just 1 mile wide. Soon the river is down to just a few hundred yards. By Minsterworth it is less than 100 yards across, maintaining this width all the way to Gloucester.

As well as this rapid decrease in the width of the river, there is also a rapid change in the depth of the river, thereby forming a funnel shape. As the incoming tide travels up the estuary, it is routed into an ever decreasing channel forming the bore wave.

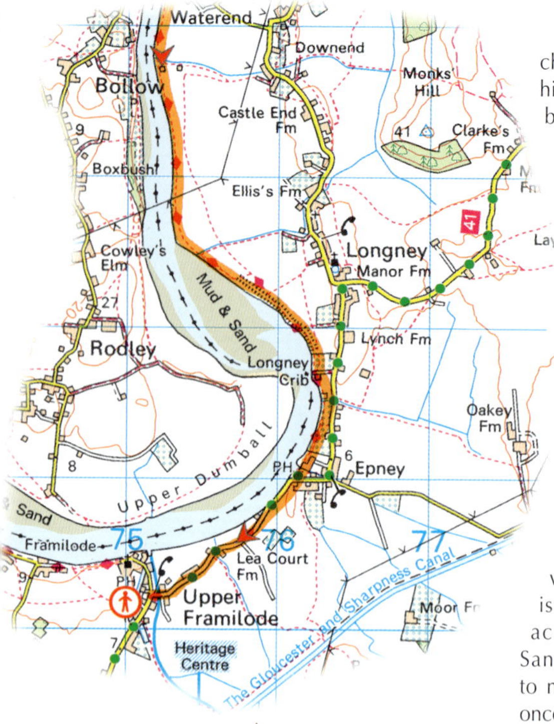

church and the wooded hills of the Forest of Dean beyond Elmore Back.

Onward from Minsterworth, the route rarely leaves the floodbank until it arrives at Watergreen, where it is diverted through an orchard at **Waterend**. Keep to the right-hand side, and on the far side cross a stiled footbridge over a ditch, and then keep right in the next field.

Onward the church in the village of **Longney** comes into view, and here the river is noticeably broader to accommodate Longney Sands, which plays host to numerous wading birds once the tide has turned.

At Bush Crib, pass a cottage and continue along the floodbank to **Longney Crib**, opposite which the river has narrowed again. A clear path leads by gates or stiles into a final section leading to the hamlet of **Epney**, where the route emerges alongside the Anchor Inn. Join the road and go forward to **Upper Framilode**, taking great care against approaching traffic – there is no footpath along this stretch of road.

Longney church

STAGE 19
Upper Framilode to Frampton-on-Severn

Start	Upper Framilode
Finish	Frampton-on-Severn
Distance	14.6km (9 miles)
Ascent	50m (165ft)
Descent	45m (150ft)

The circuit of the Arlingham peninsula is inordinately pleasing. Nowhere is the walking difficult; it's almost all on flood banks, but there is another good chance of seeing the Severn Bore (if the time is right), although here it is less impressive than further upriver.

This delightful circuit should not be missed, but there must be an awful temptation at times and in some circumstances to respond to the fact that the start and finish points are little more than a mile apart and that there is a good link between the two…you spend a few hours walking from Upper Framilode to the Gloucester and Sharpness Canal at Frampton, only to find that progress towards Severn Beach has been somewhat nominal.

The circuit, however, is a delight, and although its minimal components – flood embankments, a widening river and a few small woodlands – may not seem the most flavoursome of ingredients, they make a splendid and very relaxing dish.

FRAMILODE

Framilode consists of two settlements, Lower Framilode (also known simply as Framilode) and Upper Framilode. They lie in the parish of Fretherne-with-Saul. The River Frome enters the Severn at Upper Framilode, and the name, first recorded in the seventh century, means 'Frome crossing point', signifying a crossing of the Severn near the mouth of the Frome. There was a ferry across the Severn here, which continued in occasional use until World War 2.

Turn right along the signed road for Upper Framilode, which twists onward to reach the Severn at St Peter's Church.

THE SEVERN WAY

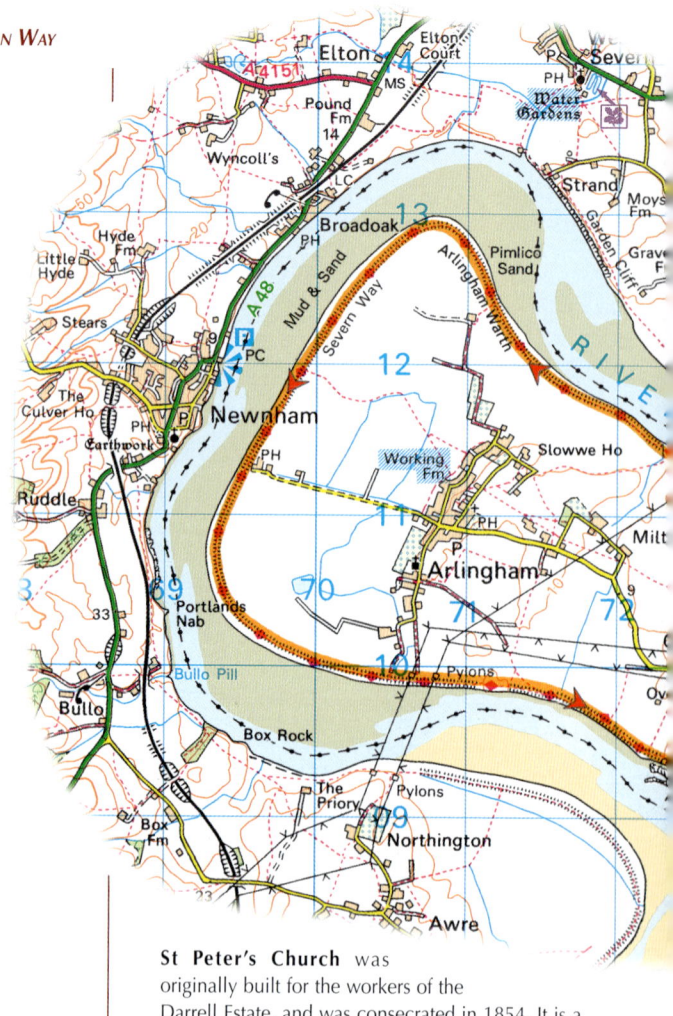

St Peter's Church was originally built for the workers of the Darrell Estate, and was consecrated in 1854. It is a pleasing example of early Victorian church design, and the youngest of five churches that make up the Severnside Parishes. The interior decoration incorporates nautical motifs, as befits a riverside church, and there are beautiful painted ceilings.

Walk past the church, go through a gate and down steps, and then on along the riverside, briefly descending to walk through **Priding**.

The name of the hamlet of **Priding** has an interesting derivation. This stretch of the Severn was once much favoured by lamprey fishermen. The local name for a lamprey – a kind of eel – was 'pride', hence Priding. It was the custom, however, that lampreys should be sent to the king, and that was what happened to many caught here.

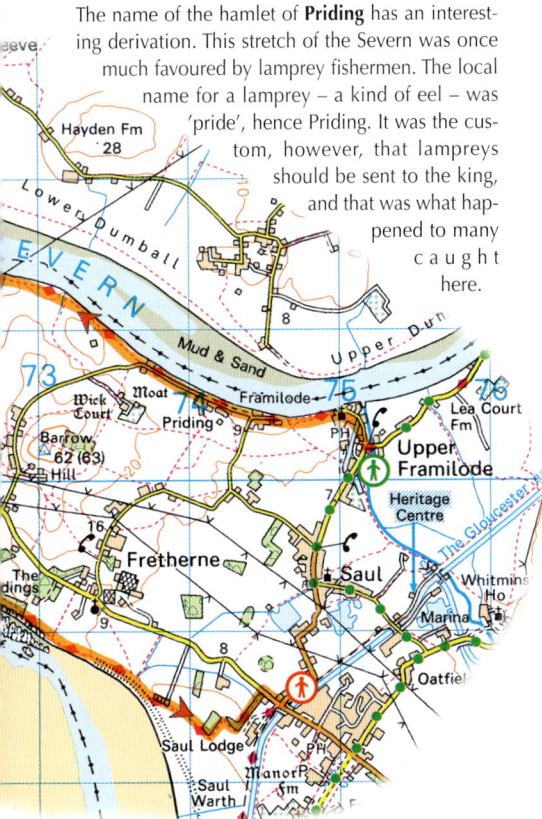

Continue along the surfaced lane as far as Priding House (currently derelict), where the lane swings to the left. Here, leave the lane by passing through a gate onto the foreshore. All that now remains is a long and gentle stroll along the embankments to the Old Passage Inn.

Watching the arrival of a small Severn Bore

There was a **crossing** at Old Passage in prehistoric times, connecting the Arlingham peninsula with iron mines in the Forest of Dean. The Romans are believed to have crossed the Severn here too, some accounts suggesting that this was done on the backs of elephants. Cattle drovers would favour this spot to cross the river, and a ferry operated here from 1802 until after the end of World War 2, when it gradually fell into disuse.

The Way continues from the inn, along the floodbank, a simple and pleasant amble. On approaching **Hock Cliff**, the path is diverted up a gentle slope into light woodland (Smith's Wood), bright in spring with wood anemone, lady's smock, celandine, bluebell and violet. The cliff itself is a Site of Special Scientific Interest (SSSI) and is protected. You can gather fossils from the shoreline and the base of the cliff but must not collect anything from the cliff itself.

Leave the woodland at a stile, and cross the end of an arable field into more woodland. On the far side, a gate gives into a small pasture. Cross diagonally right to another gate and the pasture beyond, and press on to pass the inland village of Fretherne.

Stage 19 – Upper Framilode to Frampton-on-Severn

Eventually, after following the embankment, the Way reaches a narrow tidal inlet (Hock Ditch). Cross by a footbridge, then regain the riverbank. After about 100m, leave the embankment to bear left to a waymark that directs the route alongside sewage works. Beyond the works compound, maintain the same direction along a field edge, to reach a stile that gives onto a section of boardwalk over boggy ground. At the end of this enclosed path, cross a stile and turn left to walk up the edge of a large pasture, with **Saul House** off to the right. At the top edge of the field, cross another stile, onto a narrow path along the edge of more light woodland.

At a stile on the far side of the woodland, bear left along a broad green track that eventually gives out onto a surfaced road. Turn right and walk towards the Fretherne Bridge spanning the **Gloucester and Sharpness Canal**, and there turn right onto the canal towpath. Note, immediately to the left the lovely bridge-keeper's cottage, built in the Classical style with fluted Doric columns; there are more to come on the next leg of the journey.

Walking the embankment, near Fretherne

STAGE 20
Frampton-on-Severn to Sharpness

Start	Frampton-on-Severn
Finish	Sharpness
Distance	14.4km (9 miles)
Ascent	50m (165ft)
Descent	55m (180ft)

Between Frampton and Sharpness Marina, the Severn Way simply follows the towpath of the Gloucester and Sharpness Canal; as a result, the walking is of the easiest kind, with no ascent of any note until the very end is reached. After the many and varied route idiosyncrasies that have gone in the days before, this stretch ought to be fully appreciated as the easiest of the whole route, something to take leisurely and use as an opportunity to recharge jaded batteries…and legs.

GLOUCESTER AND SHARPNESS CANAL

This splendid canal, which is the key feature of this section of the Way, was once the broadest and deepest canal in the world, and is 26.5km (16½ miles) long, 26.4m (86½ft) wide, 5.5m (18ft) deep, and could take craft of up to 600 tons.

Conceived in the canal building period of the late 18th century, the Gloucester and Berkeley Ship Canal scheme (as it was originally named) was started by Robert Mylne in 1794. In 1793, an Act of Parliament was obtained authorising the raising of a total of £200,000, but the project encountered increasing financial difficulties, to such an extent that Mylne left the scheme in 1798. Before the turn of the century, costs had reached £112,000, but only 5½ miles of the canal had been completed. Robert Mylne's role was taken over by James Dadford who had been engaged as engineer on the project in 1795, but lack of funds resulted in work being temporarily abandoned in 1800.

Between 1800 and 1810 various attempts were made to raise money to allow further building, but they came to nothing. Work resumed in 1817 under the supervision of Thomas Telford, at which time the Poor

The Gloucester and Sharpness Canal, Frampton

Employment Act meant it was possible for the company to loan money from the Exchequer Bill Loan Commission. This, along with further share issues, provided enough money to bring the scheme to completion. After these significant delays, the canal opened in April 1827. In the course of its construction the canal had cost £440,000.

From Fretherne Bridge, the towpath is joined and followed without deviation. On its journey south it passes the charming village of **Frampton-on-Severn**, one of Gloucestershire's loveliest villages and well worth a detour.

FRAMPTON-ON-SEVERN

There is a remarkably large village green, 22 acres (89,000 square metres) in size, reputedly the longest in England. By the mid-17th century this was known as Rosamund's Green, from the village's association with 'Fair Rosamund', aka Jane Clifford, one of Henry II's mistresses.

The Domesday Book mentioned the manor of Frampton in 1089, and, as if to underline the antiquity of the village, the parish church of St Mary the Virgin was consecrated in 1315 but partly dates from the 12th century.

THE SEVERN WAY

> It contains memorials to members of the Clifford family, although not to Henry's beloved Rosamund, who was poisoned by Queen Eleanor and was buried at Godstow near Oxford in 1177.
>
> Much of the village is part of the Frampton Court Estate, owned by the Clifford family, centred on the two principal houses set either side of the Green: Frampton Court, a Palladian mansion completed in 1733, attributed to the Bristol architect John Strahan, and Manor Farmhouse, of the mid-15th century. There is a designated Conservation Area around the green, including Tudor and Georgian houses, and the village also has a Site of Special Scientific Interest. Shops and pubs are a further incentive for Severn wayfarers to deviate just a little.

The route of the Way can be rejoined either by returning to Fretherne Bridge, or by continuing along the road through the village to rejoin the towpath at **Splatt Bridge** (SO 742 067).

Continuing south from Splatt Bridge, the Severn becomes visible to the west beyond low-lying salt marsh grazed by horses and wildfowl. Just before reaching the turning for Slimbridge is **Shepherd's Patch**, a place where shepherds once watched over their flocks grazing by the river. Adjoining Patch Bridge, which carries Newgrounds Lane over the canal, linking the village of Slimbridge with the Slimbridge Wildfowl and Wetlands Trust, there is the Black Shed Café/Bar and the Tudor Arms pub.

> **Slimbridge** makes an excellent deviation. It is the home of the world's largest collection of captive wildfowl, living in pens and paddocks. In addition, the site encompasses large areas of mud, marsh and meadow that form a massive wildfowl sanctuary. There are numerous well-placed hides to provide views of the birds attracted to these rich feeding grounds.

Generally uneventful walking ensues as far as **Purton**, on the approach to which the remains of a Severn bridge is encountered.

STAGE 20 – FRAMPTON-ON-SEVERN TO SHARPNESS

To bring coal to Sharpness, a railway bridge with 21 spans was built across the river, which opened in October 1879; the bridge system also featured a swing bridge to allow tall ships to pass. But on a fog-bound River Severn in 1960 the bridge was the scene of a **tragic accident** when two tanker barges, carrying 296 tons of black oil and 351 tons of petroleum spirit respectively, collided with the bridge. The collision and subsequent explosion not only caused irreparable damage to the bridge,

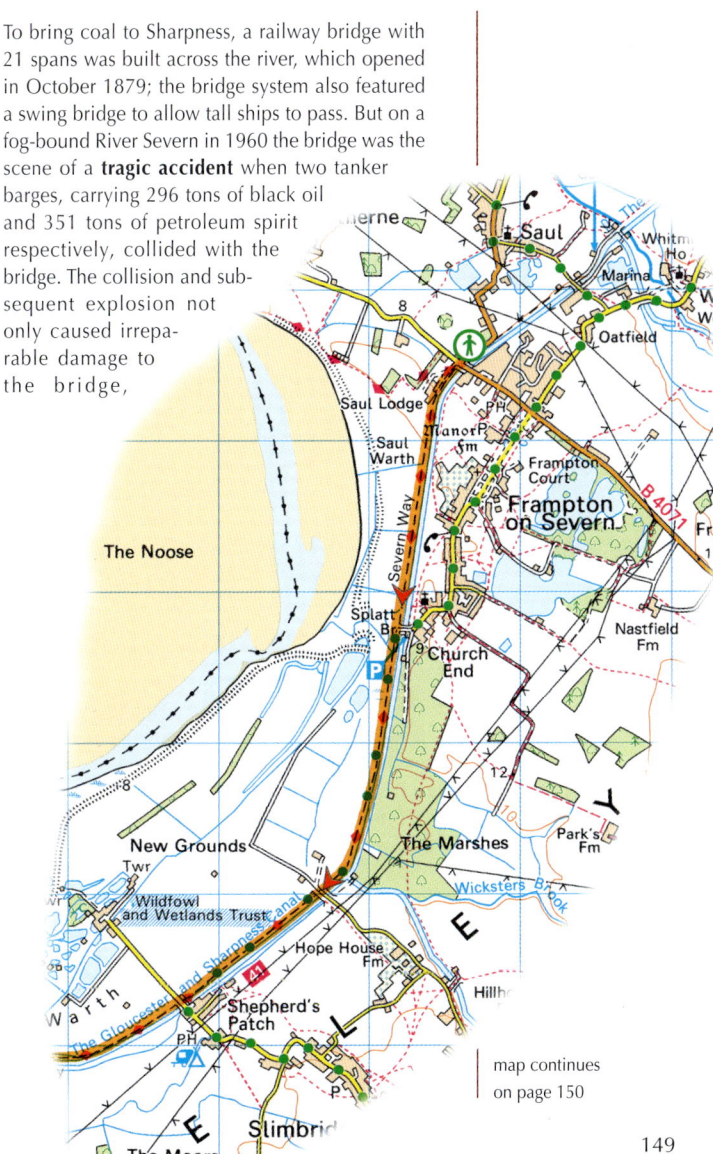

map continues on page 150

THE SEVERN WAY

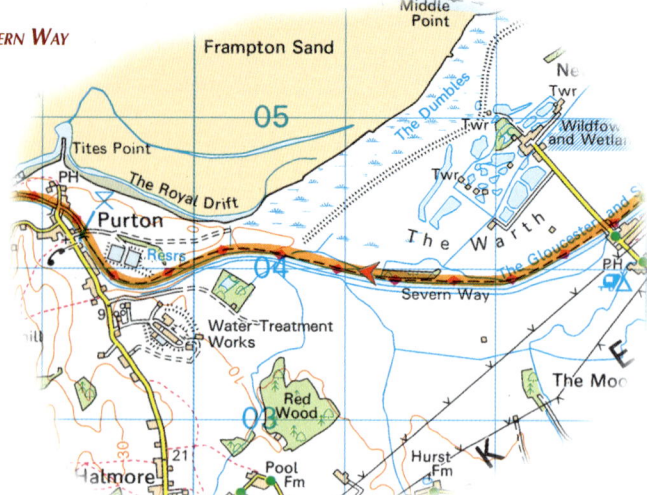

map continues on page 151

bringing down one of the upright columns and two sections of span, but also killed five members of the barges' crew. The tower that remains today used to house the steam engine that powered the swing bridge that operated here.

Here, too, is the so-called Purton Ships' Graveyard.

Memorial, Purton Ships' Graveyard

The **Purton Ships' Graveyard** is a Site of Special Scientific Interest, a place where redundant and unwanted barges were grounded and allowed to silt up between 1909 and 1965, in order to prevent further erosion of the canal bank by the River Severn. Today, with more than 80 vessels, this represents the largest collection of historic vessels in Britain.

Pressing on, only a little more of the towpath remains, and this leads round to **Sharpness** marina. Continue alongside the marina as far as a row of buildings on the right, and shortly afterwards cross a footbridge and go up steps below a car park and walk on to a surfaced lane. Follow this lane, soon descending to a road junction, and there turn left. Go forward to a T-junction, and again turn

STAGE 20 – FRAMPTON-ON-SEVERN TO SHARPNESS

River barge on the Gloucester and Sharpness Canal

left, and then take the first turning on the left and follow this to the more northerly of two bridges and onto a surfaced lane. Follow the lane as it bends right, and head towards the rows of houses that form part of **Newtown**.

Pass the Pier View Hotel and, a little further on, leave the road at a signpost, by turning right onto a path between a fence and a hedgerow. At the end of the path, cross a disused railway line and keep on in the same direction eventually to emerge on another road. Turn right, and walk about 100m to a crossroads, and there turn left towards a row of cottages at Great Western Road.

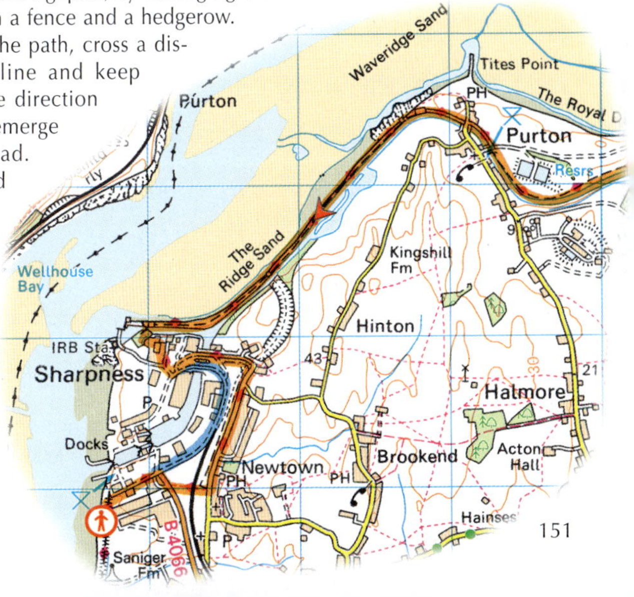

THE SEVERN WAY

Variant lower route
From the marina, continue along the breakwater and follow a clear track round to reach the foot of a brief uphill section. Ascend this, and finally emerge at the point where the original line descends from the left. Go forward likewise to a T-junction, but then stay on the lower road as it curves round and leads more directly to the crossroads beyond which the lane runs on the Great Western Road.

STAGE 21
Sharpness to Oldbury-on-Severn

Start	Sharpness
Finish	Oldbury-on-Severn
Distance	15.5km (9¾ miles)
Ascent	35m (120ft)
Descent	40m (140ft)

The walk from Sharpness to Oldbury-on-Severn should trouble no-one; it is the easiest of walking, and, if you can ignore two massive power stations, a remarkably agreeable stretch of the Way. It is all very relaxing and enjoyable, with the birdlife on the river a constant reminder of Nature's way. Wildlife is a common denominator throughout the entire walk, but, as mentioned at the end of the final section, it is hard to take in that this magnificent river began as a mere trickle high up in the mountains of Powys.

A road leads from Sharpness past the row of cottages that form the Great Western Road, and onward to join the riverbank once more at a stile on the left made from old railway lines. Over this, the familiar embankment awaits. The onward route is obvious and leads to the inlet of **Berkeley Pill**, where, of necessity, the Way deviates inland towards (but not into) the village of Berkeley, where there is a range of services.

Stage 21 – Sharpness to Oldbury-on-Severn

BERKELEY

Berkeley is midway between Bristol and Gloucester, built on a small hill above the Little Avon River, which flows into the Severn at Berkeley Pill. The Little Avon was tidal, and so navigable, for some distance inland (as far as Berkeley itself and the Sea Mills at Ham) until a 'tidal reservoir' was implemented at Berkeley Pill in the late 1960s. Berkeley was a significant place in medieval times, at which time it was a port and market town. The town is noted for Berkeley Castle where the imprisoned Edward II was murdered.

The route follows field edges alongside the watercourse and eventually reaches a minor road. Turn right, and on reaching the edge of **Berkeley Power Station**, leave the road and turn left at a signpost, to a kissing-gate, and then go forward alongside a fence to a footbridge. Continue along an enclosed path to a gate into the riverside marshland. Here, go left along the embankment, which leads, with little deviation, alongside the river.

It is the river that commands attention, and so **Severn House Farm** may not be noticed. Just beyond it, however, the Way passes from the county of Gloucestershire into South Gloucestershire (formerly Avon, and, before that, Gloucestershire).

map continues on page 154

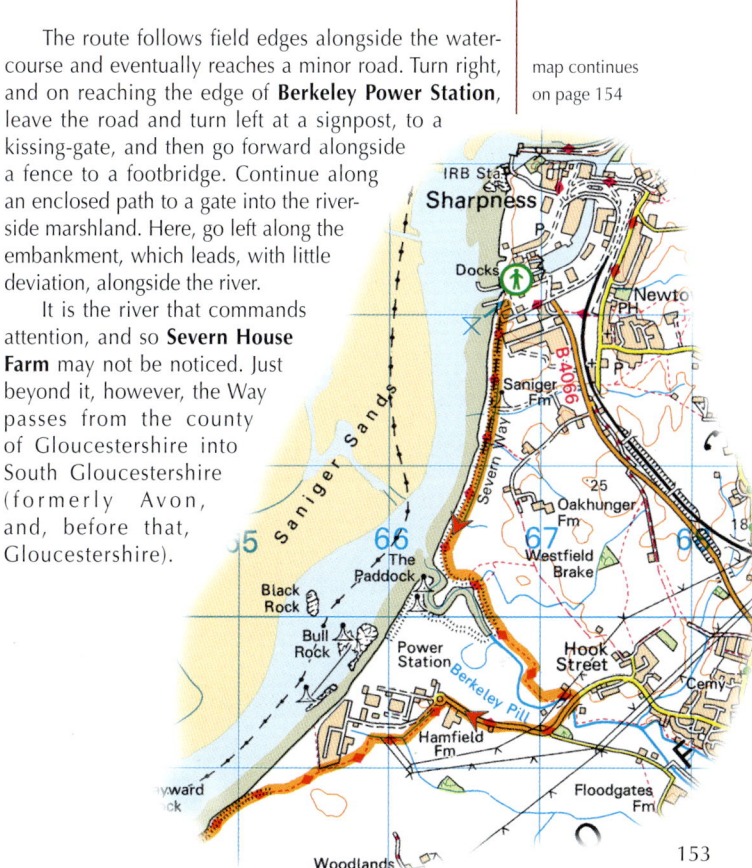

THE SEVERN WAY

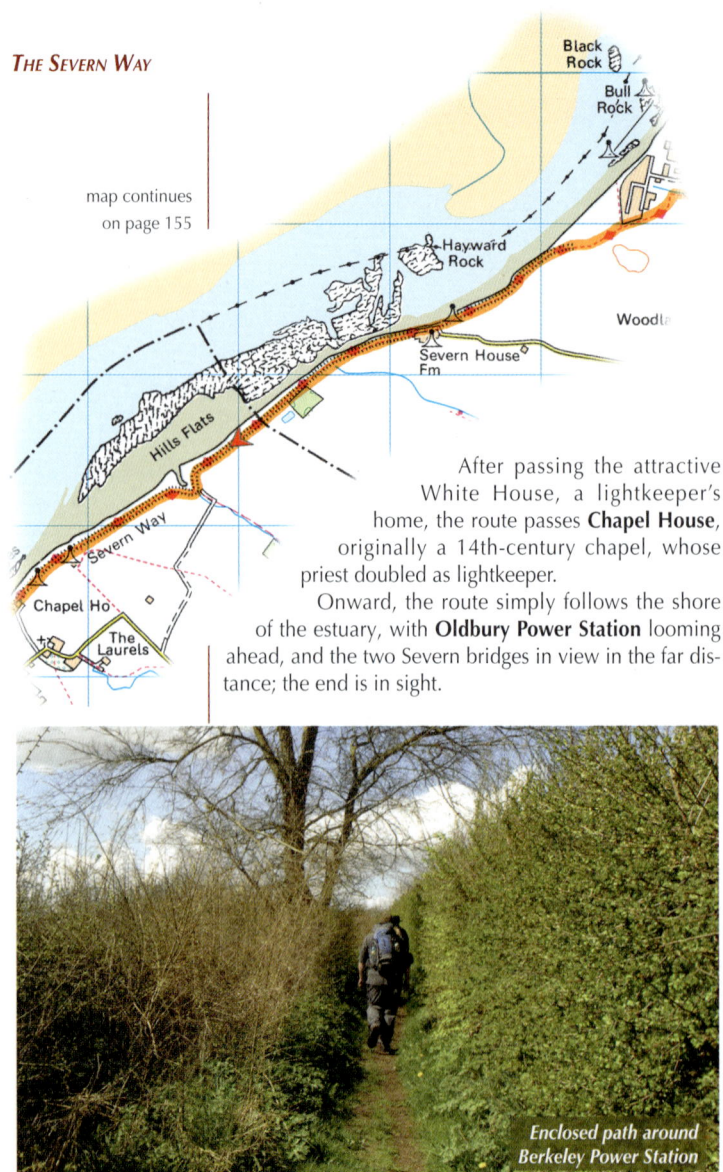

map continues on page 155

After passing the attractive White House, a lightkeeper's home, the route passes **Chapel House**, originally a 14th-century chapel, whose priest doubled as lightkeeper.

Onward, the route simply follows the shore of the estuary, with **Oldbury Power Station** looming ahead, and the two Severn bridges in view in the far distance; the end is in sight.

Enclosed path around Berkeley Power Station

STAGE 21 – SHARPNESS TO OLDBURY-ON-SEVERN

Oldbury Power Station is a twin reactor station. After 44 years of safe operation, Oldbury stopped generating in February 2012. During its lifetime, the station generated over 137.5 TWh of electricity – enough to power 1 million homes for 20 years. The station, with two reactor vessels, each containing 26,400 fuel elements, draws supplies of cooling water from the River Severn.

A clear track leads past and around the power station, and, a short way further on, the route encounters the intrusion of Oldbury Pill, where there is a small yacht club. Here, turn inland along the embankment and shortly join a surfaced lane that leads into the village of **Oldbury**.

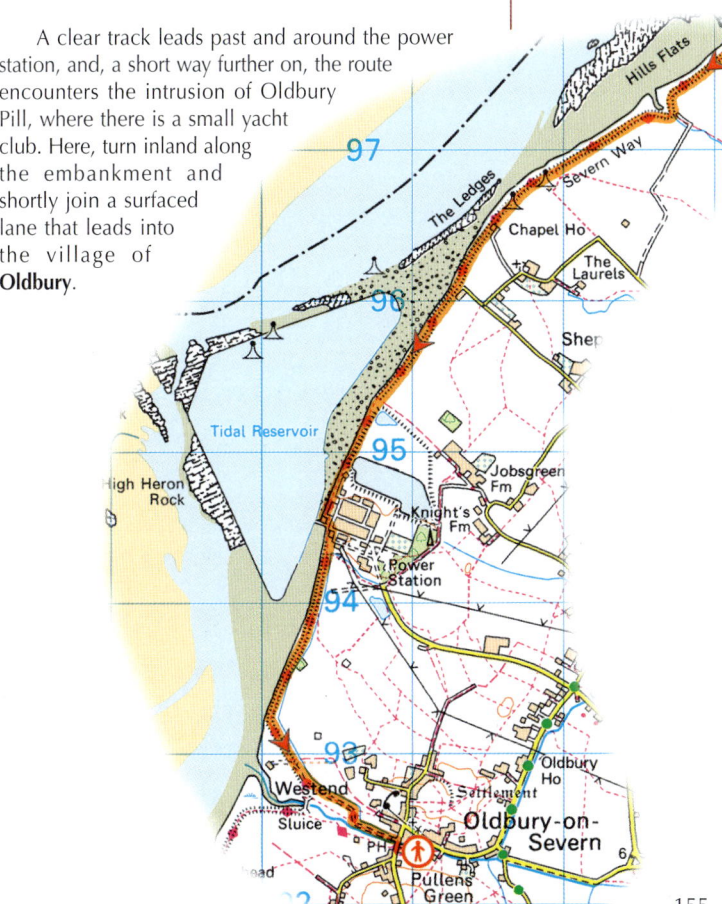

STAGE 22
Oldbury-on-Severn to Severn Beach

Start	Oldbury-on-Severn
Finish	Severn Beach
Distance	13km (8 miles)
Ascent	65m (210ft)
Descent	70m (220ft)

Oldbury Power Station is not evident from this delightful village, with its cluster of pleasant cottages and its Anchor Inn. Overlooking this small community are the remains of an Iron Age hill fort called The Toot, and St Arilda's Church, which perches imperiously on a knoll to the south – Arilda is a local saint and martyr, whose origins may lie in the fourth or fifth century.

Walk past the Anchor Inn, and shortly turn right onto a track for Ginger Bread Lodge that leads past stables and forward between paddocks. Maintain the same direction, and soon walk out to reach the Severn embankment by the mouth of Oldbury Pill. Turn left and walk the embankment, the route next being deflected inland a little at Littleton Pill. The onward route is now never in doubt, and is a pleasant and easy ramble along the embankment almost all the way to the first Severn Bridge.

Stay on the shoreline throughout this stretch until, near an electricity sub-station, it is possible to bear left at a kissing-gate and pass under a fallen tree. Beyond, the only uphill work of the day leads along the right-hand edge of a sloping pasture to a gate in a corner above. Press on along a field edge at the top of sea cliffs, and on the far side of the field, pass through another gate into light woodland and keep on to reach a concrete service road that runs around the rear of a large service area. A short way on lies a viewing area, a good place to take in the impressive bridgework that in 1966 replaced the ferry which operated across the Severn at this point, known as Old Passage.

The first Severn Bridge

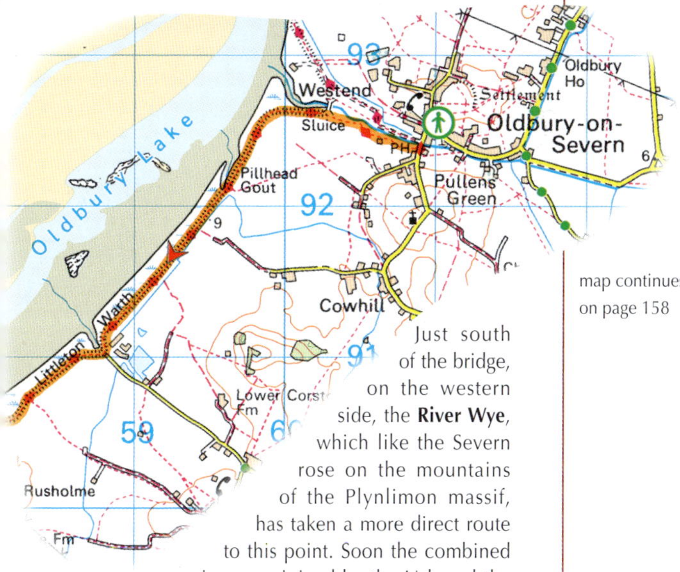

map continues on page 158

Just south of the bridge, on the western side, the **River Wye**, which like the Severn rose on the mountains of the Plynlimon massif, has taken a more direct route to this point. Soon the combined rivers are joined by the Usk and the Avon, and together flow smoothly towards the Bristol Channel and the Atlantic.

The Severn Way

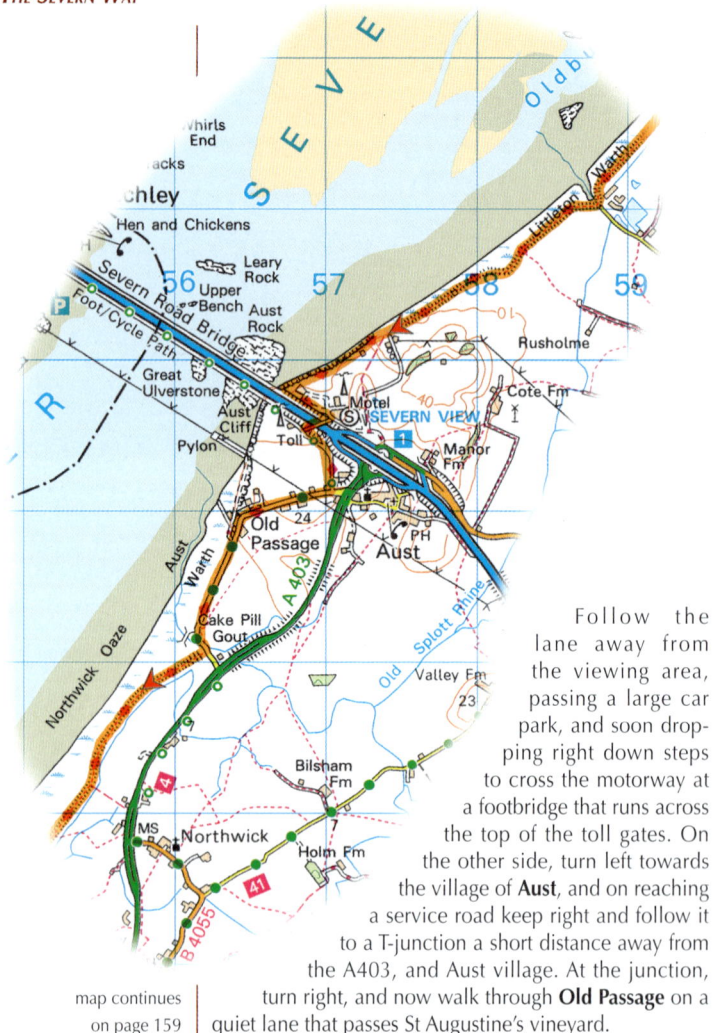

map continues on page 159

Follow the lane away from the viewing area, passing a large car park, and soon dropping right down steps to cross the motorway at a footbridge that runs across the top of the toll gates. On the other side, turn left towards the village of **Aust**, and on reaching a service road keep right and follow it to a T-junction a short distance away from the A403, and Aust village. At the junction, turn right, and now walk through **Old Passage** on a quiet lane that passes St Augustine's vineyard.

Follow the lane and then, just after crossing **Cake Pill** and before it rejoins the A403, leave the lane by turning right through a gate, continuing once more with

Stage 22 – Oldbury-on-Severn to Severn Beach

flood embankments for company. Eventually, after having crossed a sluice channel, a broad track swings to the right and comes onto a seafront wall, which soon offers a choice of a high-level walkway and a marginally lower-level parallel route, both of which rejoin further on.

Pass below the second bridge, the newest of the Severn bridges, opened in 1996, and the longest of Britain's river crossings. Now all that remains is to press on a short distance further to **Severn Beach**, the somewhat anti-climactic end to the Severn Way. Beyond, a continuing route – the Bristol Link – leads on for another day's walking into the heart of that lovely city. But for purists, the Severn Way ends here at Severn Beach with its shops, cafés and bus and rail links to Bristol.

Gazing out across the river you will find it remarkable that what began as a mere trickle high up on the moorland heights of Plynlimon has became a majestic and forceful river more than 6km (4 miles) wide.

Bristol Link: Severn Beach to Bristol

Start	Severn Beach
Finish	Quayside, Bristol
Distance	23.8km (15 miles)
Ascent	260m (850ft)
Descent	250m (820ft)
Note	The majority of the Bristol Link is waymarked specifically as the Severnway Bristol Link.

From Severn Beach go forward along the concrete pathway that continues besides the estuary from the end of the breakwater. Gradually the pathway deteriorates into a cinder track and goes through scrub to parallel the course of the railway. Stay beside the railway to a crossing point, cross with care and then follow a path to the busy **A403**. On leaving South Gloucestershire, cross Severn Road (A403) to the footway opposite, then follow National Cycling Network (NCN) Route 41 (NCN41) for 230m.

At the entrance road to **Seabank Power Station**, turn right to rejoin Severn Road and continue via a metal kissing-gate, opposite to the path that runs alongside the Severn beach to Bristol Temple Meads suburban railway line. At one point you cross a pipeline and then continue through scrub with views across the estuary to Newport and the wind turbines at Avonmouth Docks. The path bears left towards a little-used railway junction at **Hallen Marsh**.

Cross two railway lines, with care, to reach an old surfaced path and turn left to rejoin the A403 via a kissing-gate. Continue straight ahead along Smoke Lane to the first bend. Cross here into Washingpool Lane where the route rejoins NCN41; follow this tarmac path to the cul-de-sac at Cabot Park Industrial Estate, turn right and very soon left to continue on NCN41 as it follows Moorhouse Lane for 600m, through an avenue of trees.

BRISTOL LINK: SEVERN BEACH TO BRISTOL

After a road crossing, turn right to cross a wooden bridge and follow the rhynne on your left towards a large bridge over the **M49**.

map continues on page 162

A **rhyne** (Somerset), rhine/rhynne (Gloucestershire), or reen (South Wales) is a drainage ditch, or canal, used to turn areas of wetland at around sea level into useful pasture.

At a junction of rhynnes turn right and head for the motorway bridge (which has no traffic). Cross the bridge and continue into a field; follow the field edge straight on, then right and right again to reach a second wooden bridge giving onto a path (known as Lawrence Weston Road). Cross the **M5** via the new bridge to enter **Lawrence Weston**, a suburb of Bristol. Continue along Lawrence Weston Road to the T-junction with Long Cross.

Turn left and take the first right, still Lawrence Weston Road. Go straight on at a crossroads then turn right onto Broadlands Drive. About 130m after the turning take a footpath on the left, down steps. The path soon climbs uphill

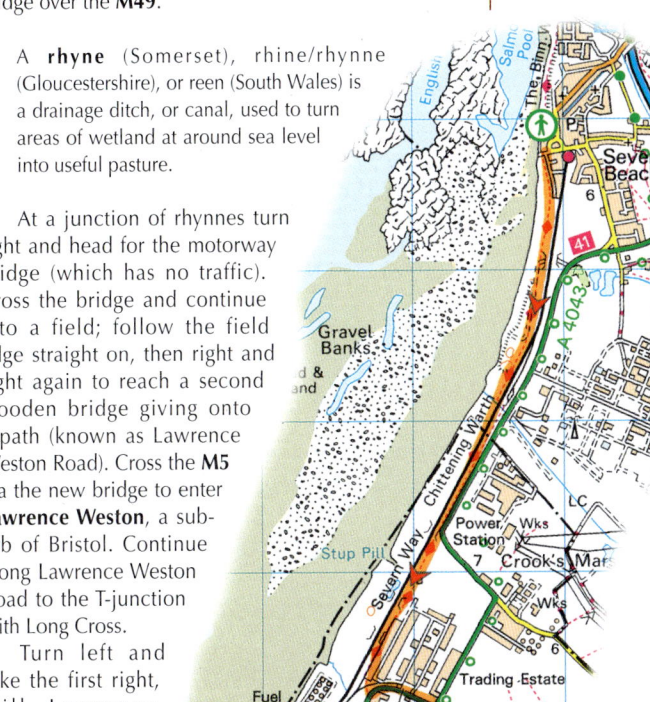

THE SEVERN WAY

between banks, on a narrow road, Fernhill Lane, and then as it levels out and swings to the left, fork right into woodland and then left along its edge, climbing up to a kissing-gate. Cross two horse paddocks diagonally then at the kissing-gate turn right to follow the fence line into Thirty Acre Wood. The route is waymarked through here and at the top of the slope the path exits into a large pasture field. From here, follow the field edge to the view across the industrial area of Avonmouth and the motorways. Here there is a path descending to the right. At the

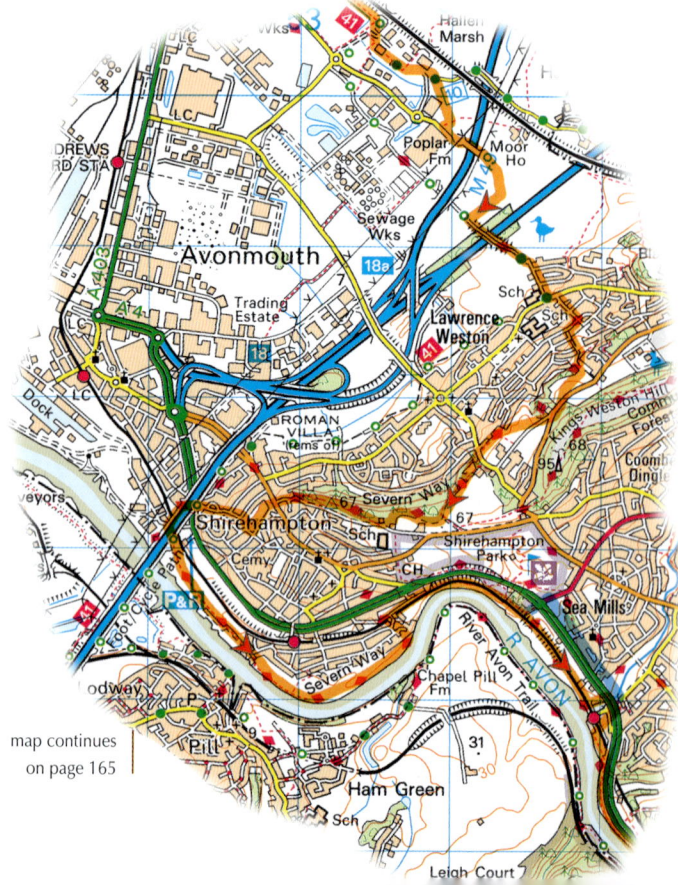

map continues on page 165

Bristol Link: Severn Beach to Bristol

T-junction turn left until you reach a road. Cross here and to the left there is a way into the woods of Kingsweston House.

As the path climbs, the view opens out to include a large stone mansion, designed by Sir John Vanbrugh in 1710. Turn right to follow the drive to the house and then along an avenue of mature lime trees. Fork right, pass a waymark and at the next junction fork left, walking through mixed woodland alive with squirrels and jays.

At the next junction, keep forward on the main path. At the next, branch left, then soon fork right, still walking through mixed woodland. When you reach a clearing, go straight across on a well-trodden path, walking now along the narrow ridge-top to a trig point. Keep forward, soon descending steps to Penpole Lane. Proceed to a T-junction.

Cross Lower High Street and take the steps opposite, and follow this path through to Beachley Walk. Continue ahead to the junction with St Mary's Road. Turn right and follow the road until you see the elevated M5 motorway. Turn left along Ermine Way and then cross the A4 (Portway) via the traffic lights. Continue under the M4 overbridge and along West Town Road, over the level crossing and then left under the bridge to the path through Lamplighters Marsh, where there are glimpses of the River Avon as it nears the mouth of the Severn.

Continue along the path to Station Road, passing the point where the Pill ferry once ran to connect with the village on the other bank of the Avon. Following alongside the river, walk beside the playing fields eventually to reach the edge of a housing estate. Continue next to the river through the open space until the last houses, and then turn left into Riverside Close, right into Nibley Road, and shortly cross a railway bridge. Turn right here and follow the path alongside allotments, towards trees.

Stay on top of the embankment to reach a set of steps down. There are glimpses of the Avon at Horseshoe Bend and views towards Bristol. At high tide boats might be travelling along the river and the same Severn Beach to Temple Meads railway line runs below.

Where the path crosses a wide pavement area, there is a viewing point. Continue via the next kissing-gate, up a set of steps and again through trees at the top of the embankment into a grass meadow. Cross the meadow, heading towards the corner nearest the railway line, descend steps, along the boardwalk, and up steps towards playing fields. At the edge of the woods, turn right towards a railway underpass. If the tide is not particularly high, go through the gates and onto the floodplain. If the tide is high, you will need to follow the high-tide variant from this point.

Follow the path towards Bristol with the railway line now on your left. Turn left under the rail and road bridges then turn right to cross the footbridge.

High-tide variant
At the first railway underpass, retrace your route a short distance to the edge of the woods and head right, up to the A4. Cross at the set of traffic lights and follow the A4 towards Bristol for 700m. Cross Riverleaze junction, pass the bus stop and before the road bridge over the River Trym turn left down a path towards the open space. At this point turn right along the paved path to rejoin the Severn Way path at the footbridge.

After crossing the footbridge, turn right to go under the road bridge towards **Sea Mills Station**. Go past Sea Mills Station, either using the path under the railway bridge or in the case of a high tide carefully crossing the level crossing at the station, and follow the old towpath past the old signal station on a very pleasant path. As it moves slightly away from the Avon there are steps up to the A4. Don't be diverted up here, stay by the river and soon the beautiful wooded cliffs of the **Avon Gorge National Nature Reserve** come into view. The path eventually leads to a flight of steps leading up to the road.

> The **Avon Gorge** provides an impressive backdrop to large parts of Bristol, an iconic landscape with the Clifton Suspension Bridge dramatically

BRISTOL LINK: SEVERN BEACH TO BRISTOL

spanning the gorge and the tidal river flowing out to the Severn Estuary.

The gorge is a very important place for geology, is home to an exceptional variety of wildlife, and supports 27 nationally rare and scarce plants, including the Bristol whitebeam, which grows here and nowhere else in the world – making it one of the most important botanical sites in the UK. It is also home to a large number of nationally rare invertebrates. Rare horseshoe bats can be found in the gorge, and peregrine falcons and ravens breed here, too.

Turn right and follow the Portway (A4) into Bristol for 2.5km (1½ miles), but take care because the pedestrian footway is also a cycleway. Once past Brunel's **Clifton Suspension Bridge** you soon see evidence of the old City docks at the large lock gates. Follow the footway, unless a gate is open to follow the dock side, under the large swing bridge to the small swing

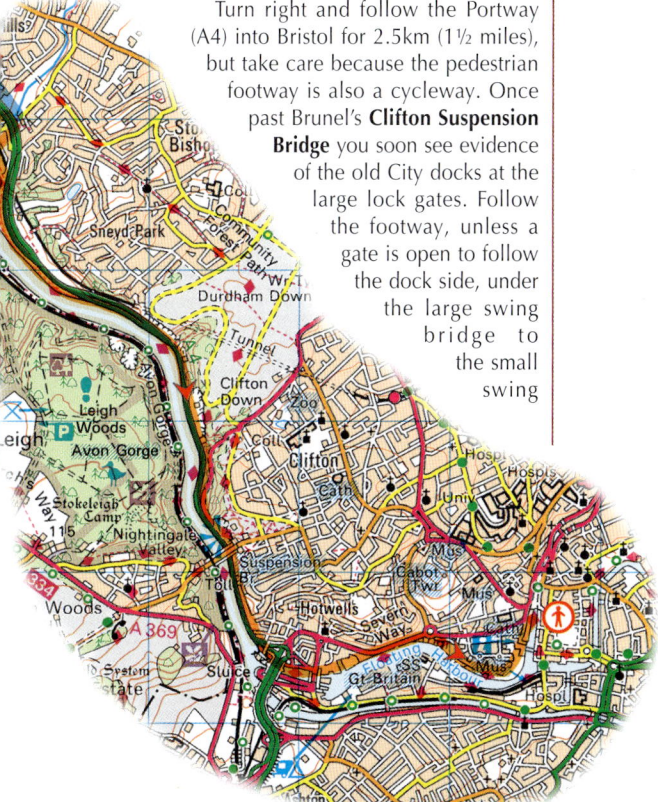

bridge, cross the road and down onto the quayside, passing in front of the Pump House pub. It is from this point onwards that you pass several ferry stops if you wish to complete your route on water to the floating harbour, opened in 1809 to allow visiting ships to remain afloat all the time. It was a busy commercial port until it closed in 1975 and has since been regenerated for leisure, commerce and residence (www.bristolfloatingharbour.org.uk). Continue with the docks to your right, past the newly developed housing; the quay's names echo the city's twinning with Porto and Hannover.

> The **SS Great Britain**, the first iron clad ship to cross the Atlantic in 1845, and the **Matthew** (if in harbour), a replica of the boat which took the Italian explorer John Cabot from Bristol to Newfoundland in 1496, are on the opposite side of the docks. There is a bust of **Samuel Plimsoll**, the man who championed the Plimsoll Line for safe loading of ships.

On approaching the floating harbour you see the old cranes on the opposite quay and the M Shed, a museum of Bristol history. Soon crossing the amphitheatre the view also opens up to include St Mary Redcliffe's spire. The Severnway Bristol link path finishes at the tourist information centre on the quayside at the E shed.

APPENDIX A
Route summary table

Stage	Start/Finish	Distance	Ascent*	Descent*	Page
	Powys				
1	Rhyd-y-benwch to the source	5.5km (3½ miles)	340m (1120ft)	65m (210ft)	23
Variant start	Eisteddfa Gurig to the source via Plynlimon	8.9km (5½ miles)	420m (1380ft)	250m (815ft)	27
2	Source of the Severn to Llanidloes	18.3km (11½ miles)	295m (960ft)	730m (2390ft)	29
3	Llanidloes to Caersws	15.5km (9¾ miles)	330m (1080ft)	375m (1230ft)	33
4	Caersws to Newtown	13.5km (8½ miles)	325m (1070ft)	345m (1130ft)	41
5	Newtown to Welshpool	23km (14½ miles)	120m (400ft)	150m (500ft)	48
6	Welshpool to Crew Green	18.3km (11½ miles)	45m (140ft)	60m (200ft)	56
	Shropshire				
7	Crew Green to Montford Bridge	13.9km (8¾ miles)	70m (230ft)	70m (230ft)	65
8	Montford Bridge to Shrewsbury (English Bridge)	10.8km (6¾ miles)	100m (320ft)	105m (340ft)	69
9	Shrewsbury (English Bridge) to Atcham	12.3km (7¾ miles)	60m (200ft)	70m (220ft)	75
10	Atcham to Ironbridge	19km (12 miles)	225m (750ft)	200m (660ft)	79
11	Ironbridge to Bridgnorth	14.8km (9¼ miles)	205m (680ft)	235m (770ft)	86

THE SEVERN WAY

Stage	Start/Finish	Distance	Ascent*	Descent*	Page
12	Bridgnorth to Upper Arley	16.5km (10¼ miles)	165m (550ft)	180m (600ft)	94
	Worcestershire				
13	Upper Arley to Stourport-on-Severn	11.9km (7½ miles)	135m (440ft)	140m (460ft)	104
14	Stourport-on-Severn to Worcester	20.5km (12¾ miles)	160m (520ft)	165m (540ft)	109
15	Worcester to Upton-upon-Severn	19.3km (12 miles)	110m (370ft)	110m (370ft)	116
16	Upton-upon-Severn to Tewkesbury	11km (7 miles)	25m (90ft)	25m (90ft)	121
	Gloucestershire				
17	Tewkesbury to Gloucester Docks	21.6km (13½ miles)	125m (410ft)	125m (410ft)	127
18	Gloucester Docks to Upper Framilode	21km (13 miles)	50m (165ft)	55m (180ft)	136
19	Upper Framilode to Frampton-on-Severn	14.6km (9 miles)	50m (165ft)	45m (150ft)	141
20	Frampton-on-Severn to Sharpness	14.4km (9 miles)	50m (165ft)	55m (180ft)	146
21	Sharpness to Oldbury-on-Severn	15.5km (9¾ miles)	35m (120ft)	40m (140ft)	152
22	Oldbury-on-Severn to Severn Beach	13km (8 miles)	65m (210ft)	70m (220ft)	156
	Total: The Severn Way	**344.2km (215½ miles)**	**2740m (8985ft)**	**3341m (10963ft)**	
	Bristol Link	23.8km (15 miles)	260m (850ft)	250m (820ft)	160

* Figures for ascent and descent are approximate.

APPENDIX B
Useful contacts

Local authorities
Powys
01597 827567
rightsofway@powys.gov.uk

Shropshire
0345 678 9000
outdoor.recreation@shropshire.gov.uk

Worcestershire
To report a problem online go to:
www.worcestershire.gov.uk, search for 'public right of way' and then click on the link to 'Report a Public Right of Way Defect Online';

or email
countryside@worcestershire.gov.uk;

or ring
01905 766493;

or write to:
Countryside Service
Worcestershire County Council
County Hall
Spetchley Road
Worcester
WR5 2NP

Gloucestershire
01452 425576
prow@gloucestershire.gov.uk

South Gloucestershire
01454 868004
rightsofway@southglos.gov.uk

Bristol
mary.knight@bristol.gov.uk

Tourist information centres
All the information centres are in a position to provide information about accommodation and transport within their area.

Powys
Newtown
Back Lane
Newtown
SY16 2NH
01686 625580

Welshpool
1 Vicarage Gardens
Welshpool
Powys
SY21 7DD
01938 552043

Shropshire
Shrewsbury
Rowleys House Museum
Barker Street
Shrewsbury
SY1 1QH
01743 281200
www.visitshrewsbury.com

Bridgnorth
The Library
Listley Street
Bridgnorth
Shropshire
WV16 4AW
01746 763257
www.visitbridgnorth.co.uk

The Severn Way

Worcestershire
Bewdley
Load Street
Bewdley
Worcestershire
DY12 2AE
01299 404740
www.wyreforestdc.gov.uk/tourism

Worcester
The Guildhall
High Street
Worcester
WR1 2EY
01905 726311
www.visitworcester.com

Upton-upon-Severn
4 High Street
Upton-upon-Severn
Worcester
WR8 0HB
01684 594200
www.visitthemalverns.org

Gloucestershire
Gloucester
28 Southgate Street
Gloucester
GL1 2DP
01452 396572
www.thecityofgloucester.co.uk

Bristol
35 High Street
Thornbury
Bristol
South Gloucestershire
BS35 2AR
01454 281638
www.visitbristol.co.uk

Transport
Inter-city coach travel
National Express
www.nationalexpress.com

Megabus.com
http://uk.megabus.com

Rail travel
National Rail Enquiries
www.nationalrail.co.uk

Local public transport information
Traveline West Midlands
0871 200 2233
www.travelinemidlands.co.uk

Traveline Cymru
0871 200 2233
www.traveline-cymru.info

APPENDIX C
Facilities along the Way

The Severn Way, although passing through sizeable towns almost daily, nevertheless has long stretches that can feel remote, and are, in any case, distant from basic facilities. The following section, while probably not comprehensive in its detail, gives an idea where facilities are available. Wherever pubs or tea rooms are encountered en route, but outside of the main centres, these are also mentioned in the text. There are remarkably few campsites.

The following entries are listed in the order in which they will be encountered, and are largely confined to the actual route, rather than at a distance from it – the exceptions being the main towns.

Llanidloes	full range of accommodation (hotels, B&Bs and camping); banks/ATMs; health centre; good range of shops, pubs and cafés, etc.
Caersws	cash machine at petrol station; small supermarket; railway station; pub (Red Lion) and hotel (Buck Hotel)
Newtown	full range of accommodation (hotels, B&Bs); banks/ATMs; health centre; railway station; bus station
Abermule (just off route)	shop
Welshpool	full range of accommodation (hotels, B&Bs and camping); banks/ATMs; health centre; good range of shops, pubs and cafés etc. Tourist Information Centre (will arrange accommodation for whole of Severn Way)
Pool Quay	pub (The Powys) offering B&B
Crew Green	pub (Fir Tree Inn), and Brookhouse Farm B&B
Melverley	pub (Tontine Inn) offering accommodation
Pentre	pub (Royal Hill Inn): no accommodation, but campsite at rear of pub (01743 741772)
Montford Bridge	pub (Wingfield Arms): no accommodation, but campsite at rear of pub (0785 3934379)
Shrewsbury	full range of services, including rail and bus services
Atcham	pub/hotel (Mytton and Mermaid)
Wroxeter	hotel (Wroxeter Hotel)
Cressage	pub (The Eagles)
Ironbridge	full range of services, but no railway

The Severn Way

Coalport	pub (The Boat Inn) on right bank, and pub across bridge on left bank; also youth hostel
Bridgnorth	full range of services, including railway on Severn Valley Railway
Hampton	pub (Unicorn Inn), seasonal refreshments at station
Stanley	pub (Ship Inn)
Upper Arley	post office/shop, tea shop, toilets (near car park)
Bewdley	full range of services, and on Severn Valley Railway
Stourport-on-Severn	full range of services
Worcester	full range of services
Upton-upon-Severn	full range of services
Tewkesbury	full range of services
Ashleworth	village shop and post office (with cashback facility), bakery, licensed tea room and telephone kiosk book swap
Maisemore	pub (White Hart)
Gloucester	full range of services
Epney	pub (Anchor Inn)
Old Passage	pub/hotel/restaurant (Old Passage)
Frampton-on-Severn	shops and pubs/hotels
Slimbridge	Black Shed café/bar at canal bridge, along with pub (Tudor Arms)
Sharpness (Newtown)	Pier View Hotel
Oldbury-on-Severn	pub (Anchor Inn)
Severn Beach	full range of services, and railway line to Bristol

LISTING OF CICERONE GUIDES

BRITISH ISLES CHALLENGES, COLLECTIONS AND ACTIVITIES
Cycling Land's End to John o' Groats
Great Walks on the England Coast Path
The Big Rounds
The Book of the Bivvy
The Book of the Bothy
The Mountains of England & Wales:
 Vol 1 Wales
 Vol 2 England
The National Trails
Walking the End to End Trail

SHORT WALKS SERIES
Short Walks Hadrian's Wall
Short Walks in Arnside and Silverdale
Short Walks in Nidderdale
Short Walks in the Lake District: Windermere Ambleside and Grasmere
Short Walks in the Surrey Hills
Short Walks on the Malvern Hills

SCOTLAND
Ben Nevis and Glen Coe
Cycle Touring in Northern Scotland
Cycling in the Hebrides
Great Mountain Days in Scotland
Mountain Biking in Southern and Central Scotland
Mountain Biking in West and North West Scotland
Not the West Highland Way
Scotland
Scotland's Mountain Ridges
Scottish Wild Country Backpacking
Skye's Cuillin Ridge Traverse
The Borders Abbeys Way
The Great Glen Way
The Great Glen Way Map Booklet
The Hebridean Way
The Hebrides
The Isle of Mull
The Isle of Skye
The Skye Trail
The Southern Upland Way
The Speyside Way Map Booklet
The West Highland Way
The West Highland Way Map Booklet
Walking Ben Lawers, Rannoch and Atholl
Walking in the Cairngorms
Walking in the Pentland Hills
Walking in the Scottish Borders
Walking in the Southern Uplands
Walking in Torridon, Fisherfield, Fannichs and An Teallach
Walking Loch Lomond and the Trossachs
Walking on Arran
Walking on Harris and Lewis
Walking on Jura, Islay and Colonsay
Walking on Rum and the Small Isles
Walking on the Orkney and Shetland Isles
Walking on Uist and Barra
Walking the Cape Wrath Trail
Walking the Corbetts:
 Vol 1 South of the Great Glen
 Vol 2 North of the Great Glen
Walking the Galloway Hills
Walking the John o' Groats Trail
Walking the Munros
 Vol 1 – Southern, Central and Western Highlands
 Vol 2 – Northern Highlands and the Cairngorms
Winter Climbs: Ben Nevis and Glen Coe

NORTHERN ENGLAND ROUTES
Cycling the Reivers Route
Cycling the Way of the Roses
Hadrian's Cycleway
Hadrian's Wall Path
Hadrian's Wall Path Map Booklet
The C2C Cycle Route
The Coast to Coast Cycle Route
The Coast to Coast Walk
The Coast to Coast Walk Map Booklet
The Pennine Way
The Pennine Way Map Booklet
Walking the Dales Way
Walking the Dales Way Map Booklet

NORTH-EAST ENGLAND, YORKSHIRE DALES AND PENNINES
Cycling in the Yorkshire Dales
Great Mountain Days in the Pennines
Mountain Biking in the Yorkshire Dales
St Oswald's Way and St Cuthbert's Way
The Cleveland Way and the Yorkshire Wolds Way
The Cleveland Way Map Booklet
The North York Moors
The Reivers Way
Trail and Fell Running in the Yorkshire Dales
Walking in County Durham
Walking in Northumberland
Walking in the North Pennines
Walking in the Yorkshire Dales: North and East
Walking in the Yorkshire Dales: South and West

NORTH-WEST ENGLAND AND THE ISLE OF MAN
Cycling the Pennine Bridleway
Isle of Man Coastal Path
The Lancashire Cycleway
The Lune Valley and Howgills
Walking in Cumbria's Eden Valley
Walking in Lancashire
Walking in the Forest of Bowland and Pendle
Walking on the Isle of Man
Walking on the West Pennine Moors
Walks in Silverdale and Arnside

LAKE DISTRICT
Bikepacking in the Lake District
Cycling in the Lake District
Great Mountain Days in the Lake District
Joss Naylor's Lakes, Meres and Waters of the Lake District
Lake District Winter Climbs
Lake District: High Level and Fell Walks
Lake District: Low Level and Lake Walks
Mountain Biking in the Lake District
Outdoor Adventures with Children – Lake District
Scrambles in the Lake District – North
Scrambles in the Lake District – South
Trail and Fell Running in the Lake District
Walking The Cumbria Way
Walking the Lake District Fells –
 Borrowdale
 Buttermere
 Coniston
 Keswick
 Langdale
 Mardale and the Far East
 Patterdale
 Wasdale
Walking the Tour of the Lake District

DERBYSHIRE, PEAK DISTRICT AND MIDLANDS
Cycling in the Peak District
Dark Peak Walks
Scrambles in the Dark Peak
Walking in Derbyshire
Walking in the Peak District – White Peak East
Walking in the Peak District – White Peak West

SOUTHERN ENGLAND

20 Classic Sportive Rides in South East England
20 Classic Sportive Rides in South West England
Cycling in the Cotswolds
Mountain Biking on the North Downs
Mountain Biking on the South Downs
Suffolk Coast and Heath Walks
The Cotswold Way
The Cotswold Way Map Booklet
The Kennet and Avon Canal
The Lea Valley Walk
The North Downs Way
The North Downs Way Map Booklet
The Peddars Way and Norfolk Coast Path
The Pilgrims' Way
The Ridgeway National Trail
The Ridgeway National Trail Map Booklet
The South Downs Way
The South Downs Way Map Booklet
The Thames Path
The Thames Path Map Booklet
The Two Moors Way
The Two Moors Way Map Booklet
Walking Hampshire's Test Way
Walking in Cornwall
Walking in Essex
Walking in Kent
Walking in London
Walking in Norfolk
Walking in the Chilterns
Walking in the Cotswolds
Walking in the Isles of Scilly
Walking in the New Forest
Walking in the North Wessex Downs
Walking on Dartmoor
Walking on Guernsey
Walking on Jersey
Walking on the Isle of Wight
Walking the Dartmoor Way
Walking the Jurassic Coast
Walking the South West Coast Path and Map Booklets:
   Vol 1: Minehead to St Ives
   Vol 2: St Ives to Plymouth
   Vol 3: Plymouth to Poole
Walks in the South Downs National Park

WALES AND WELSH BORDERS

Cycle Touring in Wales
Cycling Lon Las Cymru
Glyndwr's Way
Great Mountain Days in Snowdonia
Hillwalking in Shropshire
Hillwalking in Wales – Vols 1&2
Mountain Walking in Snowdonia
Offa's Dyke Path
Offa's Dyke Path Map Booklet
Ridges of Snowdonia
Scrambles in Snowdonia
Snowdonia: 30 Low-level and Easy Walks – North
Snowdonia: 30 Low-level and Easy Walks – South
The Cambrian Way
The Pembrokeshire Coast Path
The Pembrokeshire Coast Path Map Booklet
The Severn Way
The Snowdonia Way
The Wye Valley Walk
Walking in Carmarthenshire
Walking in Pembrokeshire
Walking in the Brecon Beacons
Walking in the Forest of Dean
Walking in the Wye Valley
Walking on Gower
Walking the Severn Way
Walking the Shropshire Way
Walking the Wales Coast Path

INTERNATIONAL CHALLENGES, COLLECTIONS AND ACTIVITIES

Europe's High Points
Walking the Via Francigena Pilgrim Route – Part 1

AFRICA

Kilimanjaro
Walks and Scrambles in the Moroccan Anti-Atlas
Walking in the Drakensberg

ALPS CROSS-BORDER ROUTES

100 Hut Walks in the Alps
Alpine Ski Mountaineering
   Vol 1 – Western Alps
   Vol 2 – Central and Eastern Alps
The Karnischer Hohenweg
The Tour of the Bernina
Trail Running – Chamonix and the Mont Blanc region
Trekking Chamonix to Zermatt
Trekking in the Alps
Trekking in the Silvretta and Ratikon Alps
Trekking Munich to Venice
Trekking the Tour of Mont Blanc
Walking in the Alps

PYRENEES AND FRANCE/SPAIN CROSS-BORDER ROUTES

Shorter Treks in the Pyrenees
The GR10 Trail
The GR11 Trail
The Pyrenean Haute Route
The Pyrenees
Walks and Climbs in the Pyrenees

AUSTRIA

Innsbruck Mountain Adventures
Trekking in Austria's Hohe Tauern
Trekking in Austria's Zillertal Alps
Trekking in the Stubai Alps
Walking in Austria
Walking in the Salzkammergut: the Austrian Lake District

EASTERN EUROPE

The Danube Cycleway Vol 2
The Elbe Cycle Route
The High Tatras
The Mountains of Romania
Walking in Bulgaria's National Parks
Walking in Hungary

FRANCE, BELGIUM AND LUXEMBOURG

Camino de Santiago – Via Podiensis
Chamonix Mountain Adventures
Cycle Touring in France
Cycling London to Paris
Cycling the Canal de la Garonne
Cycling the Canal du Midi
Cycling the Route des Grandes Alpes
Mont Blanc Walks
Mountain Adventures in the Maurienne
Short Treks on Corsica
The GR5 Trail
The GR5 Trail – Benelux and Lorraine
The GR5 Trail – Vosges and Jura
The Grand Traverse of the Massif Central
The Moselle Cycle Route
The River Loire Cycle Route
The River Rhone Cycle Route
Trekking in the Vanoise
Trekking the Cathar Way
Trekking the GR20 Corsica
Trekking the Robert Louis Stevenson Trail
Via Ferratas of the French Alps
Walking in Provence – East
Walking in Provence – West
Walking in the Ardennes
Walking in the Auvergne
Walking in the Briançonnais
Walking in the Dordogne
Walking in the Haute Savoie: North
Walking in the Haute Savoie: South
Walking on Corsica
Walking the Brittany Coast Path

GERMANY

Hiking and Cycling in the Black Forest
The Danube Cycleway Vol 1
The Rhine Cycle Route
The Westweg
Walking in the Bavarian Alps

IRELAND
The Wild Atlantic Way and Western Ireland
Walking the Wicklow Way

ITALY
Alta Via 1 – Trekking in the Dolomites
Alta Via 2 – Trekking in the Dolomites
Day Walks in the Dolomites
Italy's Grande Traversata delle Alpi
Italy's Sibillini National Park
Shorter Walks in the Dolomites
Ski Touring and Snowshoeing in the Dolomites
The Way of St Francis
Trekking in the Apennines
Trekking the Giants' Trail: Alta Via 1 through the Italian Pennine Alps
Via Ferratas of the Italian Dolomites Vols 1&2
Walking and Trekking in the Gran Paradiso
Walking in Abruzzo
Walking in Italy's Cinque Terre
Walking in Italy's Stelvio National Park
Walking in Sicily
Walking in the Aosta Valley
Walking in the Dolomites
Walking in Tuscany
Walking in Umbria
Walking Lake Como and Maggiore
Walking Lake Garda and Iseo
Walking on the Amalfi Coast
Walking the Via Francigena Pilgrim Route – Parts 2&3
Walks and Treks in the Maritime Alps

MEDITERRANEAN
The High Mountains of Crete
Trekking in Greece
Walking and Trekking in Zagori
Walking and Trekking on Corfu
Walking in Cyprus
Walking on Malta
Walking on the Greek Islands – the Cyclades

NEW ZEALAND AND AUSTRALIA
Hiking the Overland Track

NORTH AMERICA
Hiking and Cycling the California Missions Trail
The John Muir Trail
The Pacific Crest Trail

SOUTH AMERICA
Aconcagua and the Southern Andes
Hiking and Biking Peru's Inca Trails

SCANDINAVIA, ICELAND AND GREENLAND
Hiking in Norway – South
Trekking in Greenland – The Arctic Circle Trail
Trekking the Kungsleden
Walking and Trekking in Iceland

SLOVENIA, CROATIA, SERBIA, MONTENEGRO AND ALBANIA
Mountain Biking in Slovenia
The Islands of Croatia
The Julian Alps of Slovenia
The Mountains of Montenegro
The Peaks of the Balkans Trail
The Slovene Mountain Trail
Walking in Slovenia: The Karavanke
Walks and Treks in Croatia

SPAIN AND PORTUGAL
Camino de Santiago: Camino Frances
Coastal Walks in Andalucia
Costa Blanca Mountain Adventures
Cycling the Camino de Santiago
Cycling the Ruta Via de la Plata
Mountain Walking in Mallorca
Mountain Walking in Southern Catalunya
Portugal's Rota Vicentina
Spain's Sendero Historico: The GR1
The Andalucian Coast to Coast Walk
The Camino del Norte and Camino Primitivo
The Camino Ingles and Ruta do Mar
The Camino Portugues
The Mountains of Nerja
The Mountains of Ronda and Grazalema
The Sierras of Extremadura
Trekking in Mallorca
Trekking in the Canary Islands
Trekking the GR7 in Andalucia
Walking and Trekking in the Sierra Nevada
Walking in Andalucia
Walking in Catalunya – Barcelona
Walking in Portugal
Walking in the Algarve
Walking in the Picos de Europa
Walking on Gran Canaria
Walking on La Gomera and El Hierro
Walking on La Palma
Walking on Lanzarote and Fuerteventura
Walking on Madeira
Walking on Tenerife
Walking on the Azores
Walking on the Costa Blanca
Walking the Camino dos Faros

SWITZERLAND
Switzerland's Jura Crest Trail
The Swiss Alps
Tour of the Jungfrau Region
Walking in the Bernese Oberland – Grindelwald, Wengen, Lauterbrunnen, and Murren
Walking in the Engadine – Switzerland
Walking in the Valais
Walking in Ticino
Walking in Zermatt and Saas-Fee

CHINA, JAPAN AND ASIA
Hiking and Trekking in the Japan Alps and Mount Fuji
Hiking in Hong Kong
Japan's Kumano Kodo Pilgrimage
Trekking in Tajikistan

HIMALAYA
Annapurna
Trekking in Bhutan
Trekking in Ladakh
Trekking in the Himalaya

MOUNTAIN LITERATURE
8000 metres
A Walk in the Clouds
Abode of the Gods
Fifty Years of Adventure
The Pennine Way – the Path, the People, the Journey
Unjustifiable Risk?

TECHNIQUES
Fastpacking
Geocaching in the UK
Map and Compass
Outdoor Photography
The Mountain Hut Book

MINI GUIDES
Alpine Flowers
Navigation
Pocket First Aid and Wilderness Medicine
Snow

For full information on all our guides, books and eBooks, visit our website:
www.cicerone.co.uk

CICERONE

Trust Cicerone to guide your next adventure, wherever it may be around the world...

Discover guides for hiking, mountain walking, backpacking, trekking, trail running, cycling and mountain biking, ski touring, climbing and scrambling in Britain, Europe and worldwide.

Connect with Cicerone online and find inspiration.

- buy books and ebooks
- articles, advice and trip reports
- podcasts and live events
- GPX files and updates
- regular newsletter

cicerone.co.uk